AF583850

88 REASONS

WHY YOU MUST NEVER SELL
YOUR HOME AT AUCTION

ALSO BY NEIL JENMAN

Real Estate Mistakes

Don't Sign Anything

Help For Home Sellers

Success Takes Character

Real Estate DOs and DON'Ts

88 REASONS

WHY YOU MUST ***NEVER SELL*** YOUR HOME ***AT AUCTION***

PLUS

7 reasons to buy at auction

NEIL JENMAN

Australia's trusted real estate author

88 Reasons Why You Must Never Sell Your Home at Auction
By Neil Jenman

Published by Authors First
25/7 Anella Avenue Castle Hill NSW 2154 Australia
Telephone (02) 9894 6265

First Published in Australia in 2022

Printed in Australia by McPhersons
Cover Design Ceridwen Dumergue
Layout by GR8 Graphics

National Library of Australia, Cataloguing-in-Publication entry:-
Jenman, Neil

ISBN 9780958651790

Respectfully dedicated to the loving memory of

ROBERT PIGOTT

(1934–2018)

DOCTOR, ARTIST, POET.

Thank you for buying many copies of my books and giving them to your home-selling friends.

And, as always, for my wife, Reiden,

whose love, loyalty and support are always there.
Thank you for marrying me.

"A healthy society shouldn't have only one voice."

Li Wenliang (1985–2020)

Punished by Chinese authorities for warning
the world about a virus that would claim his life.
His courage and love of humanity is an example for us all.

Statement regarding sales of this book

This book has been written to protect home-owners from a method of sale that hurts thousands of home-sellers every month.

All profits from the sale of this book will go towards helping to protect women from domestic violence.

HOW TO READ THIS BOOK

You do NOT have to read this book in the "normal" manner – such as starting at the beginning and reading, in page order, to the end. This is a "dip into" book. Provided you read Reason 1 (which is vital), you can skip to any reason that piques your interest. The last thing any writer wants to do is bore the reader. When you are sure that you will never sell by auction, stop reading.

As mentioned in the Introduction, this book has been written for one purpose only: To make sure, when you sell your home, that you get the **TRUE VALUE** for it.

One of the most important things you must do is resist the sales pitch of agents who try hard to persuade you to sell by auction. These agents use slick and enticing lines. They can be hard to resist.

That's why I have included 88 reasons why ***you must never sell your home by auction.***

Please read as many reasons as it takes to convince you to *never auction your home.*

This book is like a financial vaccine to protect you from the "auction virus", which can make you financially very sick.

Thank you for your trust in me. If you need further help, please email me on support@jenman.com.au.

Neil Jenman

FOREWORD

by

Frank Facciolo

Melbourne home-seller and auction-escapee

HOW I WON THE REAL ESTATE LOTTERY – AND YOU CAN TOO!

In 2020, I felt I had won a lottery. But it's a lottery any homeowner can win. Just make sure you get Neil Jenman – or his son, Alec – on your side when you sell your home. Hardly a day passes without us thinking how lucky we were to discover "Jenman".

Here's why.

When we first decided to sell our home of 30 years, we did what thousands of sellers – especially in Melbourne – do every week: We met with three local high-profile agencies and listened to their spiel. All three said the only way to sell was through auction. We went with a high-profile agent who professed to be No. 1 in Australia. I got him to reduce his commission to 1.2% provided we didn't tell anyone (because he teaches agents how not to drop their commission. I'm serious). We gave him our credit card to charge us $10,500 in advertising costs.

And then we signed up.

For auction, of course – because that's "the way everyone does it in Melbourne".

I had been receiving Neil Jenman's emails for years. I sent an email to Jenman Support asking for advice on how to find a good buyers' agent. The next thing I was talking to Neil Jenman himself. Within minutes, he told me: "You don't need a buyers' agent. I'll show you what to do and I won't charge you anything."

Well, that advice on its own saved me about $20,000 (given what buyers' agents charge).

Neil asked, "So, you've sold your house, have you?"

I told him we had signed up for an auction. I also said we'd given the agent $10,500 for advertising costs.

He told me that auction was certain to mean I would undersell my house. He told me that most people don't think much when they sell their homes; they just do whatever agents suggest. That's exactly what I had done.

I was starting to feel sick.

Neil made me realise I was being played for a mug. He said it didn't suit me to do something as stupid as throw away up to $500,000, which was likely to happen at an auction.

"But I have already signed up for auction," I said.

Neil replied: "Then cancel it. Who owns your house – you, or the agent? Take charge and tell him you refuse to get ripped off."

Neil didn't push me. He told me to think it over. He said if I wanted to use the services of Jenman Support, he would make three promises. First, he would never ask me for money. Second, he would never ask me to sign anything. And third, he would fight to protect my interests.

I asked around. I went on-line and looked up Neil Jenman. The only people opposing him were agents. His reviews from consumers were amazing. The ABC had done his life story on *Australian Story*. It's on YouTube and I urge everyone to see it. You'll see what Neil and his family have suffered in their fight to protect people like me and my family.

The next day I called Neil and said, "I am in your hands; whatever you tell me, I will do it."

His first aim was to get back our $10,500 advertising fee. I thought we had no chance because it was non-refundable. But Neil told me what to say and soon the money came back to us.

Then we cancelled the auction. The agent didn't like it, but we told him it was our house and we wanted to sell it our way.

Neil found us an agent who was trained in negotiation. An agent who did not want money up front like auction agents. An agent who said, "You only pay me when I sell your home and you are happy with the price."

Ultimately, I was more than happy. So happy to get at least $351,000 more than if I had gone to auction – maybe more than $500,000 more – that we gladly paid the new agent 2.5%. A cheap commission is not much good if the agent gets you a cheap price.

How do I know we got more than at auction? Reason 30 in this book explains it beautifully.

I was speaking with a good friend recently who told me he had just purchased a rundown house on a large block of land in Melbourne's eastern suburbs at auction. He was willing to pay $2.6 million. He bought it for $2.3 million. While my friend saved $300,000 the poor sellers lost $300,000. I now understand how this happens every week all over Australia.

Thank you, Neil Jenman, Alec Jenman, Haley Jenman and Reiden Jenman – and all your dedicated team. May you change the real estate world for the better. May the day come where, when homeowners want to sell, the first thing they do is call Jenman Support on 1800 1800 18.

Good luck to you.

Frank Facciolo

Melbourne, 2021

INTRODUCTION

If only you knew...

"If only they knew" – these are four words I say to those who are closest to me in my life. Not only do I say them, but I also think them. Almost constantly. I am referring to real estate auctions.

Every time I see a home for sale by auction, every time I see media reports saying auctions are popular, every time I see auction clearance rates, and, finally – the one that upsets me most – every time I see a report that a home sold for "hundreds of thousands of dollars above its reserve price".

When I see such a statement, I know one thing that most consumers – especially the owners of the home that apparently sold for a whopping price – don't know. The agents have got away with another near-perfect con – they **undersold** a home and fooled the sellers into believing they got the best price. And that's the essence of a quintessential con – victims don't realise they've been conned *plus* they believe they got a great deal. It goes on thousands of times each month: home-sellers thanking agents who rip them off.

If only they knew.

I have seen claims such as "Property sells for $2 million above reserve at auction". It sounds great. Of course, the sellers are thrilled. So is the agent who pocketed a commission of $220,000[1] plus collected $50,000 in advertising costs, meaning the sellers forked out $270,000. They thanked the agent. They got savagely ripped off.

If only they knew. Oh, yes, if only they knew.

But *you* are about to know because I will tell you – although the words of Mark Twain are often on my mind: "It's much easier to fool people than to convince them that they have been fooled." I hope it won't take 88 reasons to convince all homeowners that if they decide to sell by auction, they have been fooled and are likely to massively undersell their homes.

In that case – where the property sold for $2 million above reserve (the lowest price the sellers were willing to accept) – there was something else about the sale that the sellers did not know. Like most sellers, they did not know the highest price the buyers were willing to pay.

Well, get this: The buyers were willing to pay $4 million more than they did pay.

The property was a cattle station. It was as if the sellers drove away and left $4 million in the hayshed.

If only they knew.

If all home-sellers knew the truth about auctions, none would allow their homes to be sold by auction. Unless, of course, they deliberately intended to lose money. But who wants to throw away $4 million? Not you, I hope.

WHY?

Two things that agents most want to know when you sell your home are two things you shouldn't reveal: *How much you want and why you are selling.* This book will explain more.

But, right now, I will reveal my motive, the reason I am writing this book.

I want to save home-sellers from underselling their homes.

I especially want to save home-sellers who believe auction is the best way to sell for the best price. Auction is **not** the best way to get the best price – it never has been, and it never will be. Auction is the worst way to sell – any time, any place.

Agents who tell you otherwise are either lying or stupid – dishonest or incompetent.

Every week, thousands of home-sellers lose tens or hundreds of thousands of dollars by underselling their homes at auctions.

I find this appalling. It's a disgraceful indictment on an industry that is like a law unto itself where greedy, lazy and stupid agents have one aim: doing whatever is best for themselves with scant regard for the price of the sellers' homes. If agents get a commission, most don't care if a home sells below its true value.

If you are an honest and decent home-seller or buyer, I will go to great lengths to protect you. And I give you my promise that, unlike most agents, I will never put my interests ahead of yours. Nor will I ever take sides with any agent who is not doing what is in your best interests.

I have lost friendships with agents I have known for years because they treated consumers badly. Some agents expect me to side with them because they think I am "one of them".

I am not "one of them" – I never have been and never will be.

By "one of them", I mean agents who do not serve their clients but instead serve their own interests.

Although many agents have paid me for advice – and some still do – this does not mean they can buy me. I have rejected or expelled more agents from my life than all the major real estate groups. My commitment to honest consumers is not for sale – not at any price.

Most agents can't figure out my motive for helping consumers. Their response to my exposé of what goes on in real estate is to become vitriolic and hurl abuse, mistruths and accusations – either at me or about me.

The first rule within the real estate industry is to never damage the industry. The Real Estate Institute's codes of ethics[2] states that it is unethical to criticise agents or their methods. It doesn't matter if the agents' methods are unethical; it's unethical to criticise them.

It makes me laugh when agents say I "knock" them to increase my profits. They think I am like them – that my only motive is profit.

Given that, since the early 1990s, most of my income came from training agents, exposing their dodgy practices has not inspired them to attend my training courses. My revelations about real estate hurt my profits. There is no profit in speaking out in the real estate industry. But as we always say at Jenman Support: "Our best payment is the trust and appreciation from home-sellers and buyers."

As you will read in this book (Reason 60), there are too many temptations for agents – plus enormous peer pressure – to make a quick buck without caring for clients. Agents seem unable to resist the lure of the "dark side".

One of my best friends, a former agent – who now helps me find agents for sellers – is Michael Kies from Adelaide.

Michael agrees that "real estate tends to bring out the worst in people".

After nearly losing his life to leukemia in 2008, Michael sold his successful real estate agency. He wrote a real estate sales training program called "Success in Real Estate".

Like me, he began holding seminars for agents and doing coaching. Like me, he was constantly ripped off by agents who didn't pay their accounts. "I had no idea so many agents were so dishonest until they became my customers," said Michael.

He's right. In 25 years of training agents, I may have earned the biggest profits of my life, but I also suffered the biggest rip-offs of my life when agents refused to pay their accounts or cheated me for thousands of dollars. Many claimed to be my "friends". They reminded me of the saying: "With friends like these who needs enemies?"

Despite the setbacks, I persevered with my training and coaching of agents.

Until one day it all got too much. One rip-off too many probably. My dear friend Lisa Hayden, who sadly lost her life to breast cancer in January 2019, told me: “Trying to teach agents to act ethically is like trying to teach crabs to walk straight.”

And so, at the start of 2019, I did what I should have done 20 years earlier when I wrote my first book. Instead of focusing on helping agents, I decided to focus mostly on helping sellers and buyers.

I went to work at my wife’s business, Jenman Support – helping all real estate consumers, but mostly helping sellers find agents who will agree to follow 8 “protection points”. Points such as “no costs until a home is sold” and the right to “sack agents” who are not performing.

In 2020, my son Alec – who left school at the end of 2019 – came to work with me. He is often asked: “What do you like best about working with your dad?”

He always gives the same answer: “The appreciation we get from people.”

I have not written this book for agents – other than those who are smart enough to realise that the best way to have a profitable business is to do what’s best for clients.

I have written this book for home-sellers – and buyers. It is you to whom I give my loyalty. If I have done my job, you will never sell a property by public auction after you read this book.

If you appreciate my work, please do one more thing when you need to sell real estate: *CONTACT JENMAN SUPPORT BEFORE YOU CONTACT ANY AGENTS.* We will support you from start to finish – from choosing an agent to striving to help you or your agent to negotiate the best price. We do not charge sellers (we receive a fee from agents who agree not to pass this fee on to you).

The more you support us by allowing us to support you, the more people we can protect. In Australia, there are almost 8000 homes sold every week. Each homeowner will surely be better off if they contact us *before* they contact an agent.

One day when people sell a home, we hope the first thing they will do is call Jenman Support.

Thank you for buying my book.

My best wishes to you.

Neil Jenman

JENMAN SUPPORT – support@jenman.com.au

TABLE OF CONTENTS

PART 1

88 REASONS TO NEVER AUCTION

REASON 1

You get a lower price!

The first reason for not auctioning your home is the only reason you need to never auction your home: ***You will get a lower price.***

Plus, you will pay needless costs.

You will almost certainly lose a massive amount of money. And, like most sellers, you will never realise how it happened or what happened.

Indeed, the auction system is so slick that many ripped-off home-sellers thank agents who cause them to lose hundreds of thousands of dollars.

By selling at auction, you have almost no chance of getting the highest price. You have almost a one hundred per cent chance of getting a lower price.

And because most sellers don't know they lose, there is no publicity about such massive financial disasters. It's as if someone steals from home-sellers who never miss the loss.

So yes, the number one reason you should **never** sell a home by public auction is that you get a lower price. Auction destroys the true value of your property.

If you believe what has just been said – and, please believe it, because it's true – and you make a promise to yourself (and your loved ones) right now that you will ***never sell a home by public auction,*** you don't need to read further. Of the 88 reasons in this book, surely selling for a lower price is enough to turn you off selling by auction.

If you need more reasons, 87 others follow.

REASON 2

The "competitive" myth

Agents love to tell sellers that an auction is a competitive environment. They say all the buyers are brought together, and the competition forces the price up.

Buyers do not buy real estate because of the method it is sold. It is not an auction that makes buyers buy a home, it's the fact that they love the home.

Buying a home is an emotional event. When buyers love a home, many will pay a huge price for that home – often well above its current value.

For example, a home might be worth, say, \$1.5 million, but if buyers love the home, it's not unusual for them to pay \$2 million or more.

And yet, at auction, it's common for these buyers to buy homes at hundreds of thousands of dollars below the price they are willing (and eager!) to pay.

Why?

Because auctions are not so much competitive. They are comparative.

At an auction, all buyers get to compare bids offered by other buyers.

And so, if a buyer has a limit of \$2 million, but bidding is rising in amounts of \$100,000 and the price reaches \$1.5 million, the buyer with the \$2 million limit will increase a bid by \$100,000 which takes it to \$1.6 million.

If there are no other bidders to push the highest bidder higher, the home is *undersold* by \$400,000 below what the winning buyer was willing to pay. This happens at *most* auctions!

Auctions are not competitive, they are comparative. And that means a lower price.

REASON 3

Sellers and agents have different agendas

Here's the problem for home-sellers: You and the agent have different agendas.

Your agenda is to sell your home for the best price. This should be non-negotiable. Why would you purposely sell your home *below* its best price? That would be like accepting a lower salary in your job. Such an attitude does not make sense.

You must look after your family's finances.

But whereas your agenda is to sell your home for the *best price*, the agent's agenda is to *sell your home.*

At any price.

As soon as possible.

With auctions it's easy for agents to mislead sellers into believing they get the best price. It's also easier for agents to get a sure sale at any price.

The agent must share your agenda of selling for the best price. Don't get caught in their agenda of a quick sale at any price. Don't auction.

REASON 4

Auctions suit agents not sellers

To understand auctions, you must understand agents.

Most agents are only interested in commissions. They get commission when a sale happens. Before a sale, agents must get a listing (a home for sale).

In real estate, the "sell" is not to buyers. Most homes *sell* themselves. Agents just stand at a front door – or, if it's quiet, take a nap on the sellers' lounge[3].

The real "sell" in real estate is selling owners to list their homes. The best way to sign up (list) sellers is to promise a great price. Once sellers sign up, agents must convince them to accept less than they were promised when they signed up.

Auctions are a great way for agents to mislead sellers into thinking they will get the best price. Once signed up, agents are trained at convincing sellers to lower their price "expectations". The "sell" is always on sellers. Selling them to list. Selling them to reduce. Selling them to accept the best offer at an auction, no matter how low. Selling them to "listen to the market".

Auctions do not push prices up; that's an illusion. Agents perpetuate this illusion and fool sellers into thinking auctions are the best way to sell and get the highest price.

The opposite is true: Most homes (at least 90%) are **undersold** at auction[4].

Auctions do not suit sellers, not even close.

But auctions suit agents.

Agents push auctions because auctions are the fastest and easiest way for agents to get their commission.

REASON 5

Hopeless negotiators

Agents who push auctions are hopeless negotiators. If they were good at negotiation, they would not use a method that undersells properties.

All agents will tell you they are great negotiators. But ask them for an example of how they negotiate. If you are not impressed – which you are unlikely to be – don't hire them.

Of course, agents who push auctions will tell you about one great sale of a home that sold for a million dollars above the reserve price. When they tell you such a story – and now that you know that even when homes sell at auction for more than their reserve, they almost certainly sold below the buyer's highest price – here's what to do:

Ask the agent for details of that great sale where, due to the agent's supposed great negotiation skill, the home sold for a million dollars (or whatever amount) above its reserve price. Then glance at your phone. Look up and say to the agent: "The buyers who bought that home for that big amount over the reserve price, they were willing to pay another $375,000. So, really, although it may have sold above its reserve, it was undersold by $375,000."

The agent will immediately ask: "How do you know that?"

And this where you "check-mate" the agent.

You reply by saying: "How do you **not** know that?"

The best way to get the best price for your home is to hire a competent negotiator. Most agents are hopeless at negotiation; but auction agents are the worst negotiators, by far.

To know more about what makes a great negotiator, please go to jenman.com.au and download the booklet *The 42 Rules of Modern Real Estate Negotiation.*

REASON 6

Auctions are built on lies, deception & manipulation

Real estate auctions are based on lies, half-truths and deception.

To make the auction system work, agents tell two major lies. First, they promise sellers a high price. Second, they mislead buyers into believing the home will sell for a low price.

With enough pressure exerted on both sellers and buyers, a sale is made. The lies are blamed on "the market".

A recent poll revealed that 95% of people do not rate agents highly for ethics and honesty[5]. It begs the question: *Why do so many homeowners place their greatest financial asset with someone they don't trust?*

Perhaps home-sellers think auctions are a proven method which has been around for thousands of years. So, surely an auction will work for us?

But the entire auction system is an illusion that relies on lies, half-truths, planned deceit, and psychological manipulation to persuade home-sellers to sell at any price, no matter how low.

Agents who say auctions get the best price either don't know how to get the best price or don't want to get the best price. They are either incompetent or dishonest. The effect is the same – a lower price for the sellers. Never sell your home with such agents.

Find an honest and competent agent. They do exist.

REASON 7

Total loss of control

Agents love control. “Controlled listings” are their greatest desire. A controlled listing is one where the agent – not the seller – has control.

No sellers are more controlled than auction sellers.

No agents revel in control more than auction agents. Their hubris is notorious. The way they laud it over buyers you’d think the agents owned the homes.

The biggest stress in life occurs when we lack control. Agents like it this way. They know what to say to increase the stress on sellers and make them pliable. Stress “softens” sellers.

When stress is high, reason vanishes. It becomes more important to relieve stress than achieve the original goal. With real estate auctions, removal of stress for sellers often takes priority over the price. “Oh, just sell it – and end this psychological torture.”

As one auction trainer wrote in his book for agents: “It is your job to keep them nervous[6].”

Don’t lose control. Reject auction as a method of sale.

You’ll have less stress and more money.

REASON 8

Consumer rights denied

On 15 March 1962 (World Consumer Rights Day), President John Kennedy called on the United States Congress to introduce legislation which gave consumers four fundamental rights.

Fast forward 60 years. If you are a homeowner and you are being advised by an agent to sell your home by auction, these four rights are not available to you. On the contrary, some are deliberately denied to you.

The first right is the RIGHT TO SAFETY. There is no more dangerous way to sell a home than auction. From the danger of burglars "casing" your home at inspections to the danger of far more costs than needed, to the almost certain danger that your home will be undersold – probably massively so – these are dangers you probably know nothing about.

The second right is the RIGHT TO BE INFORMED. As an auction seller, not only are you not informed, but you are deliberately misinformed.

If you sell by auction, you will be subject to a raft of lies from when you first meet an agent to when your home gets undersold by tens or hundreds of thousands of dollars.

The third right is the RIGHT TO CHOOSE. With auctions, not only is choice denied to you, so is control. If you auction your home, you are controlled by a dodgy agent.

The fourth right is the RIGHT TO REDRESS. If something goes wrong – such as if your home sells well below the price you were quoted – you have no right to redress.

At auction, the basic consumer right of a GUARANTEE is missing – for both the sellers and the buyers.

REASON 9

The law won't help you

Real estate agents routinely break consumer protection laws. They have almost no fear of being prosecuted – for two reasons: First, every agent seems to be breaking laws under the Fair Trading Acts or the Competition and Consumer Act and, second, the authorities rarely prosecute agents. Even laws under the Crimes Act, most notably "obtain a financial advantage by deception" – the very definition of fraud – are blatantly breached.

The first time I appeared on television talking about auctions, I said, "The auction system is a fraud." A well-known Melbourne agent said, "I take great offence to that remark[7]." He gave his usual pitch about his integrity and longevity in real estate. This agent – like all auction agents – had been misleading sellers and buyers for years. He was never challenged by authorities. Even after the program aired on national television with hundreds of thousands of viewers, this agent – along with many agents – kept telling lies. It was more than 20 years before his agency's conduct became too brazen to ignore. Government inspectors examined 22 of his company's auctions and found that all involved massive deception. The Federal Court imposed a penalty of $880,000[8]. That got the attention of agents. For a while. But soon, they were brazenly breaking laws again. As they are today – and every day. No fear of attack or penalties. A law unto themselves. As they have been for years.

When a Melbourne barrister sued an auction agent for underselling his home by at least $200,000, the case was dismissed. The judge said the barrister was well educated; he should have known better. Everyone knows auctions are a "farce"[9].

The boss of the Real Estate Institute said the judge did not understand auctions.

Understand this: Auctions are riddled with deceit, and consumers have little or no redress.

REASON 10

Hostility and anger do not get a better price

Moving home is one of the most stressful events in life[10]. The most stressful way to sell or buy a home is auction. Agents revel in this atmosphere (especially male agents) with many writing in their "profiles" how they "enjoy the excitement of auctions".

Why compound the stress by using the most stressful way to handle a stressful event? Because stress is a planned part of the auction process, that's why. Agents are taught to keep people nervous[11]. It may seem dramatic, but the psychological pressure on buyers and sellers with the auction system is often likened to torture.

Auctions are confrontational.

Auctions don't just cause stress; they breed fear, resentment, hostility and anger. These emotions should be avoided when negotiating, not encouraged. Provided you want the best price. If you want a sale at any price, use auction with its high-pressure emotions.

To get the best price, sellers should choose a method where people are treated with dignity and respect. Courtesy is not only a good strategy, it's common decency. Showing consideration for others is called "doing the right thing". It makes them pleased to do business with you.

The hostility and anger created at auctions is never the right way to treat people. It gets them off-side. Confrontation does not lead to the best result.

The way to get the best result is to treat people well.

And that means avoiding auctions.

REASON 11

Auction destroys the value of your home

The value of a property is widely accepted as: "Whatever a willing buyer is prepared to pay[12]."

Let's say a buyer is prepared to pay $2 million for your home. And yet, that buyer buys your home at auction for $1.6 million. Obviously, you have **not** got the true value of your home.

It doesn't matter if you "hoped" to get $1.5 million (which was your "reserve" price).

It doesn't matter if you may be *delighted* to have got $1.6 million.

It doesn't matter if the agent says you got "$100,000 above your reserve".

It doesn't matter if you or anyone knew the buyer was willing to pay $2 million.

All that should matter is that you **UNDERSOLD** your home.

If you sell your home for $1.6 million to a buyer who was ready and willing to pay $2 million, you have lost $400,000 from its value. It probably means you hired a poor negotiator, such as an agent who recommended auction.

The true value of your home is what a willing buyer will pay for it. Anything less means you have not protected the value of your home.

Auction destroys the value of your home.

REASON 12

Auctions **focus** on the wrong price

When selling a property, there are two important prices.

The first is the sellers' lowest price. The second is the **Buyers' Highest Price** (BHP).

There is a famous saying: "Whatever you focus upon grows." So, what should competent agents focus upon – increasing the buyers' highest price or decreasing the sellers' lowest price?

With auctions, agents are obsessed with lowering the sellers' price.

They have a psychologically manipulative way to achieve this aim.

It's called "conditioning". It's their pre-planned method of discovering the sellers' lowest price.

But agents have no plan to discover the buyers' highest price.

Agents claim that auctions get the best price, but they focus on the sellers' lowest price. They never ask buyers to disclose their best price. Hard to believe, isn't it?

If agents wanted to sell homes for the best price, they would take their focus off the wrong price, namely the sellers' lowest price, and put it on the right price, the buyers' highest price.

To achieve that goal, agents would have to come clean, ethically and honestly.

And that would mean doing what all sellers should do – reject auctions.

REASON 13

Never reveal your lowest price

If you want to sell your home for the best possible price, ***never reveal your lowest price.***

This is a Golden Rule in real estate. Yet nearly all home-sellers break it. This is why homes are undersold by hundreds of thousands of dollars.

The people most responsible for home-sellers breaking this rule – and therefore damaging the value of the home – are those employed to get the best price: the agents.

Agents can't get the best price by forcing sellers to reveal their lowest price. Yet, the first question most agents ask home-sellers is: "How much do you want?"

Sellers should give one well-rehearsed answer to the "how-much-do-you-want" question: "We want the best price, whatever it might be. But first we want to find the agent most likely to get us the best price at the lowest cost."

Or shorten it and say: "We want the best agent who can get us the best price."

The reason you hire an agent is to get you the highest price.

When you think about it – which many sellers don't – think about this: What possible reason could any agents have for wanting to know your lowest price?

Remember this:

If you reveal the lowest price you will accept, it will soon become the highest price you get.

REASON 14

Agents don't care about selling for the best price (**BHP!**)

Auction agents do not care about selling properties for the highest price. If they did care, they would not recommend auction.

Most sellers believe agents who say auctions are the best way. It does not occur to sellers that the well-presented and well-spoken agents can be incompetent or dishonest.

To agents, getting the best price is secondary to making a sale at *any* price. Agents only care about getting the sellers' reserve (lowest price) low enough to make a sale. As agents know, it's easier to make sales at lower prices.

Consider this: agents call the sellers' lowest price the "reserve price".

What do agents call the buyers' highest price?

Nothing. They don't even have a name for it.

Yes, the entire focus of agents is on the sellers' lowest price.

HELP TIP: As most agents do not have a name for the buyers' highest price, you can give it one. From now on, refer to the buyers' highest price as the **BHP**. Auctions do not get sellers the BHP.

REASON 15

Mathematically impossible

Anyone who believes auctions are the best way to sell for the best price must have failed maths at school. Here is a test of your "Auction Maths". Children are welcome to participate.

AUCTION MATHS TEST

Five buyers attend an auction.

The highest prices of each buyer (which are **not** disclosed) are as follows:

Buyer 1 = $2 million.

Buyer 2 = $2.1 million.

Buyer 3 = $2.3 million.

Buyer 4 = $2.37 million.

Buyer 5 = $2.65 million.

The "reserve" price (the sellers' lowest price) is $2.25 million.

Please answer the following three questions:

Q1: *Given that, at an auction, each buyer can see how much the other buyers are bidding, what will be the likely selling price of this home at auction?*

Answer: ....

Q2: *As the reserve was $2.25 million, how much did the home sell ABOVE reserve?*

Answer: ....

Q3: *As the BHP for Buyer 5 was $2.65 million, by how much was the home undersold?*

Answer: ....

SUMMARY: As happens at most auctions, the home sells for a high price, well above its reserve price, which is what everyone sees and the media reports. What no one sees, and few people realise, is that these "success stories" are mathematical disasters for sellers who lose hundreds of thousands of dollars and never know it. Auctions are a near-perfect con. Victims suffer massive losses, but believe they enjoyed a gain. They tell friends about their "auction success". The myth spreads like a financial virus and wipes millions of dollars from the value of homes. If you want the best price, don't auction.

Q1: $2.38 million

Q2: $130,000

Q3: $270,000

REASON 16

Please explain, Mr Agent

There is a simple reason auctions do not get the best price (as agents claim), yet many agents are either too stupid to realise the reason or too dishonest to admit it. That reason is this: *The best price comes from buyers.* But, as mentioned, agents focus on the sellers' lowest price, not the buyers' best price. How can you get what you don't know? How do you get something if you don't ask for it? So, to use a quote made famous by a female politician when she was asked if she was xenophobic, let's make a request of Australia's auction-pushing agents:

TO ALL AGENTS WHO CLAIM THAT
AUCTIONS GET THE BEST PRICE,
"PLEASE EXPLAIN!"

- *"There are three buyers at my auction. Buyer 1's best price is $1.5 million and Buyer 2's best price is $1.6 million and Buyer 3's best price is $2 million.* ***Please explain*** *to me how you can ensure my home sells for $2 million, which is the best price any of the buyers can pay?"*
- *"There are two bidders competing against each other at an auction. The first bidders have a maximum price of $4 million. The second bidders have a maximum price of $5 million. When the first bidders bid $4 million (which is their limit) and the second bidders then bid $4.1 million (which is $900,000 below the best price they can pay),* ***please explain*** *how you get the other $900,000 and therefore do as you claim happens at auctions – get the 'best price'?"*
- *"You recommend I sell by auction. You claim it's the way to get the best price. Please explain how you can get the best price at an auction when your focus is on the reserve, which is my lowest price, and not on the buyers' highest price."*

REASON 17

Agents rarely meet buyers!

Before an auction, agents meet sellers to discuss the reserve price. Agents want to know the lowest price the sellers will accept. Agents urge sellers to set a "realistic reserve".

But why?

How does it help sellers get the best price if they lower their lowest price?

When agents talk about being "realistic", surely it would be more "realistic" in helping sellers to get the highest price if agents met with buyers to discuss their highest price.

Auction agents rarely meet buyers to discuss the highest price.

That's why auctions don't get the highest price.

STORY: An agent who promotes auction, also promotes himself as a good negotiator. He was kind enough to speak with me (on the record in a taped call). I told him that being a good negotiator and being an auction proponent didn't make sense. Good negotiators do not recommend a method that undersells homes. At auctions, agents only know the price the sellers will accept, **not** the price the buyers will pay.

He agreed.

Then he said: "Before each auction we qualify all buyers and discover their highest price."

Well, that's good, but do you ever have bidders you've never met turning up at your auctions?

Oh yes, he replied. We call them "auction fairies".

Anyone who believes auctions get the best price must also believe in fairies.

REASON 18

Agents don't even ask!

Agents often say: "How are we supposed to know what buyers are prepared to pay? We are not psychic." Er no, not psychic. But not too smart either.

So, let's explain this slowly (for the benefit of such agents).

To discover the highest price buyers are prepared to pay, do what you do to discover the lowest price sellers are prepared to accept: *ask them*.

If you don't know how to achieve that task, you should not be in sales. And you most certainly should not be entrusted with the sale of a family's biggest financial asset.

As all professional salespeople know, a major requirement of selling is getting to know prospective customers. It's called "QUALIFYING".

At real estate auctions, agents often don't meet the buyers until after they have bought!

By being too lazy to "qualify" buyers, auction agents short-change sellers by massively underselling their homes.

And these sellers are paying upwards of $20,000 for a *salesperson* to *sell* their home?!

Auction agents are *not* salespeople, not even close. They are not even "order-takers" (one of the worst labels that can be given to a salesperson).

They don't even ask buyers the most basic sales questions: "How much have you got to spend?"

Most auction agents are lazy and incompetent. They destroy the value of homes they are entrusted to sell.

REASON 19

Auctions start low

Agents love to say, "At auctions, the price goes up. With normal sales, the price goes down."

Anyone who knows anything about negotiation knows that one of the most important rules to getting the best price is: *Start high!*

If you want a high price, never start with a low price.

The reason prices go up at auction is because they *start low.*

The aim at auctions is to get the buyers up to the sellers' lowest price. And then, most times, the bidding stops. It's then that agents put pressure on sellers to lower their reserve price.

This is when many sellers "crack" under pressure and sell their home for less than the agents promised they'd get at auction. Best price? Not likely.

For agents, auctions are a typical case of "do the least we need to do" to make a sale.

It's not whether bids go up or down that's important. What's important is where bids stop.

When bids start low, sellers begin the negotiation from a position of weakness. This is another breach of negotiation protocol. This is why skilled negotiators reject auctions. They are horrified that auction agents put sellers in such a weak position.

Bidding starts low with the aim of reaching the sellers' lowest point. And then it's all over. Another undersold property.

The negotiation rule is simple: The higher you start, the higher you finish. By starting low, you finish lower. That's the most common auction formula.

REASON 20

Reserve does ***not*** protect sellers

Agents use slick lines to convince sellers to choose auction. One of their favourites is: "You can't undersell at auction because your reserve price protects you."

That's more auction nonsense.

Who protects sellers from agents who descend on them at the auction?

When bidding stops below the reserve, agents gather around sellers and pressure them like they have never been pressured. Drop the reserve. Do it now. This is what the market is saying.

It's part of the agents' plan; it's built in to the auction system.

One auction trainer taught agents about "crunching vendors at the auction":

"You shouldn't worry if the reserve seems a little high because when the bidding slows down, the reserve can be lowered immediately to the amount of the highest bid ... **Bingo! Another Sale.**" [Bold inserted by the trainer].

Later, this same trainer says: "Whatever the highest bid is (unless it's completely ridiculous), you should urge them to take it."

This trainer tells agents that they need a "Plan of Attack" for sellers at auctions.

Sellers need a Plan of Defence. The best is simply this: Do not auction.

REASON 21

Auctions are a "conditioning" method

Most agents have the same problem: Sellers want too much money. But if agents tell sellers the truth about the price of their homes the agents won't be selected.

Agents feel they have no choice but to lie to sellers to win listings. They can worry about getting the price down later once the sellers have signed up and can't escape.

Auctions give agents the perfect excuse to **not** mention a specific price, yet still suggest that an auction will create a *huge* price. Agents make comments such as, "Let's see what the market says." They sprout stories of record results at auctions. The message is clear – this can happen to you. And the big lie: Auctions get the best price.

Once sellers sign up for auction, agents use the word "market" at every chance.

The market this … The market that … This is what the market is saying … You need to listen to the market …

Or their most idiotic phrase: *You need to meet the market.* As if the market is another person. That's close to true. Agents tell lies, and the market is their alibi.

"Don't blame me, it's the market," say the agents. But why is the market always worse after sellers sign up? It's all to do with "CONDITIONING", which means bombarding sellers with bad news and negative feedback about their homes.

The Real Estate Institute of Australia published *The Real Estate Office Manual.* It stated that "Auctions are the fastest and best conditioning method".

That's the big reason agents push auctions – they are the best way to condition sellers.

REASON 22

Lowball buyer feedback to create a "fake market"

When sellers sign up for auction, so much of what the agent says seems reasonable. Agents use well-rehearsed lines learned over years at seminars and meetings. In a few years, auction agents morph into something resembling stage actors.

At all stages of the "auction campaign" there is zero attention given to what agents promised the sellers, namely, to "get the highest price". It's all about getting sellers to lower their price. As just shown, this is done with a crafty process called "conditioning" or, as some agents call it, "managing expectations". Whatever name, the aim is the same: Get sellers to accept a reserve low enough to make a sure sale.

Sellers are told that "the market" will determine the price. The market, of course, means the buyers. Agents tell sellers they will get comments on what buyers say about their home.

Today's buyers are savvy; they know that agents will give their comments to the sellers. As all buyers want to buy cheaply, many give "lowball" offers. It's what buyers hope to pay. Buyers know the agents will pound sellers with these "lowball" figures.

The agents ask everyone who inspects the home – from sticky-beaks to neighbours to serious buyers – the price-dropping question: "Is there any price at which you would buy this home?" When such a question is asked of someone who is not interested in buying the home unless it is an absolute bargain, that person will give a "lowball" price or offer.

This "lowballing" is presented to owners by agents who say: "This is what the market is saying." Word spreads that the reserve may be low. Hence, a bigger turnout at the auction. "What a great crowd," agents say. The message is clear: We will get the "market price" today.

Huge pressure is applied to sellers if their home fails to reach reserve. Sellers are told "This is what the market is saying."

By encouraging lowball offers, agents do terrible damage to the value of sellers' homes. They have created a fake low market.

The sellers are under extreme pressure. The conditioning process and lowball offers have softened them up. The agents say, "We always told you, from the beginning, that the market sets the price. Well, this is what the market is saying."

The sellers don't realise that the agents have been getting the buyers' *lowest* offers. Not once have the agents attempted to discover the *highest* offer the buyers are prepared to make. The lowest offers are presented as "the market price"; the sellers are told "This is the highest the market will pay".

Rubbish – it's the lowest the sellers will accept.

Thanks to lowball offers, the conditioning and pressure about "the market", sellers may undersell their homes by hundreds of thousands of dollars.

This is the nature of real estate auctions where homes are massively undersold.

REASON 23

Dummy offers

A big part of "conditioning" involves frighteningly low offers before the auction. The earlier the offers, the sooner the sellers are softened up ("conditioned").

Low offers put pressure on sellers to lower their reserve price. And here's the "rule of thumb" for agents: If the low offer doesn't frighten sellers, it's not low enough. It's the "mule and the mallet" theory – it gets attention[13].

In many cases, however, low offers are fiction. They are dummy offers.

Indeed, the lower the offers, the more likely they are to be fake. For two reasons. First, few buyers would dare insult sellers with such a low offer and second, if sellers accept a dummy offer, the agent has some explaining to do. It can be hilarious to hear agents trying to bumble their way out of explaining why they can't find a buyer who made an offer. How do you find someone who doesn't exist?

DUMMY OFFERS ARE COMPANY POLICY.

A salesperson at one large Melbourne agency, where the goal is "auction everything", revealed how salespeople give home-sellers a low fake offer after the first open inspection[14].

This is not a suggestion; it's an order. Every seller gets a fake low offer.

But what if the open house is a big success? What if there are several keen buyers? Surely, there is no need for the dummy offers in these cases.

But here's the problem for agents: "If vendors think lots of buyers are interested, they get greedy and increase their reserve price."

It is just as important to hide good news as to manufacture fake bad news. The worse the news – and the more of it – the more chance the reserve price will be low. Nothing makes a sale at auction more certain than a low reserve.

Start the bad news early and keep it coming. That's how "top agents" do it. Australia's self-described number one real estate trainer[15] tells agents to: "Go ugly early."

The modern term for the "conditioning process" is "managing expectations". If agents delay bad news, it's harder to convince sellers to lower their "expectations".

The strategy for these fake low offers is to make them at least 20% below the lowest price the sellers expect. If they expect $1.5 million, they get a dummy offer of $1.2 million.

These dummy offers achieve their purpose – they soften up the sellers. If the highest bid at the auction is above the dummy offers, sellers are likely to accept it – even if it is well below what they originally expected.

Don't play the dummy game. Every time agents hit sellers with an offer from buyers, sellers should ask to meet the buyers.

Dummy offers are just another way agents convince sellers to lower their prices at auctions.

REASON 24

Dummy bidding

Real estate auctioneers are liars. Aside from the hyperbole, lying is essential. Lies keep an auction moving. Lies in auction are like spark plugs in an engine – they create momentum.

The lie at the heart of auctions is the dummy bid.

Years ago, the then-CEO of the Real Estate Institute of Victoria[16] told the media that he didn't know what was meant by "dummy bidding". A journalist[17] explained it – "Someone standing in the audience pretending to be a real bidder and they're not."

The CEO replied: "Auctions have been around for a long time." And so have lies.

As one agent quipped: "How can we have an auction with one bidder?"

Years ago, before the outcry over dummy bidding, which was always illegal, agents were brazen about it. Some agents invoiced sellers for planting dummy bidders in the crowd[18].

Like so much with auctions, reality is different from appearance. The purpose of dummy bidders is not, as sellers believe, to inflate the price, it's to make sellers believe the dummies (who never bid over the reserve) are real bidders.

Therefore, when the dummies stop bidding – below the price the sellers expect – the sellers lower their reserve and sell, no matter how low the price.

Sellers should be warned: If an agent hints at doing something dodgy, get rid of the agent. Dodgy agents do not discriminate. They are dodgy with everyone.

REASON 25

Dummy reviews

When Penny tried to sell her home, the agent concocted a fake buyer story to persuade her to sign another selling agreement for a further three months. Penny reluctantly agreed. Almost immediately the (fake) sale crashed. The agent told Penny not to worry. It will be sold again.

Penny was suspicious. She investigated ("snooped", the agent called it) and discovered that the supposed sale was a sham. The agent had invented a dummy buyer and gone to great lengths to concoct a long story – something about living overseas and funds coming via Asia. (**WARNING**: *The more detailed a story, the more likely it is fake.*)

Penny was furious. She fired the agent. But the agent told Penny she could not cancel the agreement. Penny protested that she had been tricked into re-hiring the agent.

Penny originally chose this agent after reading glowing reviews. So, Penny went on-line and wrote a negative review including her suspicions about past reviews. "Either these reviews are fake," wrote Penny, "or these sellers have been conned."

Within 30 minutes, Penny's review was deleted. The agent replaced Penny's bad review with a fake good review – all in Penny's name, describing the agent as "wonderful". Penny was in a nightmare.

It got worse. The agent's lawyer sent Penny a demand for $10,000 for "pain and suffering" caused to the agent.

Fake reviews are the modern real estate scam. Agents pay the reviewing website, which means agents have control – that's why, even though 95% of the public distrust agents, on some websites (which should be called FakeMyAgent), 95% of the public love agents.

REASON 26

Underquoting = Undersold

Most sellers who are persuaded to auction are told: "Quoting a lower price attracts more buyers. We push them up at the auction. Leave it to me; I have been doing this for years."

The agent convinces sellers that a fake low quote leads to a better price. But the opposite happens. Quoting a fake low price leads to a real low price.

An agent who admits to cheating buyers is almost certain to cheat sellers.

Underquoting the likely selling price *does* attract more buyers. But, unfortunately for the sellers, it attracts buyers *at* the underquoted price.

Agents then say to sellers: "This is what the market is saying."

To which sellers should reply: "But you attracted the wrong market because you promoted the home at the wrong price."

Remember: You must attract buyers who can afford the price you want.

REASON 27

Lost money & broken hearts

Thousands of buyers are burned at auctions.

They spend hundreds of dollars on inspection reports, surveys, and legal advice checking out homes. When a home sells above the price the agent quoted them, they lose money. This can easily be a couple of thousand dollars. They get their hearts broken and their wallets walloped. It's one of the most unreported and distasteful aspects of auctions.

Of course, when buyers miss out, agents say this is more proof that auctions get high prices.

But that's *not* the reason. Agents lie to buyers by saying they have a "good chance", knowing they have no chance. This is how agents get buyers to an auction. When the sale price exceeds the agents' quotes, the agents blame "the market". But the market doesn't set the reserve which is above the agents' quote to buyers.

Agents don't care how many buyers lose money at an auction. Many agents pocket thousands of dollars in kickbacks on building reports.

If you wonder why governments don't legislate to make sellers provide necessary reports, you've just found the reason. Corruption and self-interest.

Not only are buyers hurt with this corrupt system, so are sellers[19]. Buyers get sick of losing money because agents lie about the likely price.

This is just another reason why many buyers refuse to consider homes being auctioned.

REASON 28

But wait - more costs!
feed the greed

Auctions give agents a perfect chance to slug sellers for all sorts of spurious charges.

If you are selling a home for millions of dollars, what does a few hundred dollars matter? Or even a few thousand? Incidental costs seem small. Auction agents love to say: "One extra bid will pay for [name needless expense]!"

Every cost you incur in selling your home should be seen in isolation. If you are selling a home for millions of dollars, what's another $250 for an "administration fee"? See it in isolation. $250 is five fifty-dollar notes. Don't feed the greed. These are your dollars.

When agents "load up" different costs for different reasons (most you never considered), you can be sure of one fact: At best, the agent is greedy. At worst, a thief. To charge for items that are needless or, worse, do not exist, is a form of theft.

Auctioneer's fee – up to a thousand dollars. Soon it will be $2000 (on the "whatever-we-can-get-away-with" principle). Get this – it is payable if the auction proceeds or not. Even if the agency has its own auctioneer or uses a rent-a-show-pony. Money for nothing; they love it. Floor plans, photography (plus the drone). And a copywriting fee: $250 – $500 for illiterate agents. And you'll love this one: Chinese translation fee: $200. Or the coffee wagon at the auction. One agent charged $800 for an Elvis impersonator. And, of course, look for the "plus GST" instead of "incl GST". You are a milking cow. Instead of milk, they squeeze you for every dollar.

Auctions: *Never so much charged to so many for so little.*

Don't feed their greed. Auctions are a big cost for little effort by incompetent agents.

REASON 29

The best you get at auction is the **second-best** price

If you sell at auction, the best price you will get is slightly more than the second-best price.

To be sure, the second-best price is often a good price. But it's not the best price.

Indeed, the second-best price may be more than expected, even well above the reserve price – which, of course, as a seller, is your lowest price.

If you get a few hundred thousand dollars extra, of course you will be happy.

But here's a question that's never asked (because agents don't want auctions exposed as the sham they are): No matter how far a bid is above the reserve – even, say, $400,000 – it's rarely the best price.

If the buyer is prepared to pay *another* $400,000, *would you prefer that amount?*

Of course you would.

For example: If your reserve price was $3.5 million and the bidding reached $3.9 million – which is $400,000 above your reserve – it feels like you are getting $400,000 EXTRA.

But if the highest bidder was prepared to give you *another $400,000* it would bring the final price to $4.3 million, meaning $800,000 EXTRA.

Much better, right?

But, at a public auction you never know how much the highest bidder is prepared to pay. Or, as agents often say behind-the-scenes: "The buyers had more in the tank."

So sure, in this example, the sellers would get $400,000 *above* their reserve if bidding reached $3.9 million.

But if the highest bidders had another $400,000 "in the tank", the sellers would miss out on the next $400,000.

This means they'd get the second-best price. As happens at auctions.

This is the great problem with auctions: The highest bidder only pays a little bit above the second-highest bidder, not the highest they are willing to pay.

The difference between the best price and the second-best price is often hundreds of thousands of dollars. Sometimes millions of dollars. That's how much sellers often undersell at auctions.

Do you want the maximum value, or do you want to slash the value and give a huge discount to strangers, people you have never met and will never see again?

If you want to sell your home for the best price, don't auction it.

REASON 30

"Public" is the problem!

It's not so much an auction that causes homes to be undersold, it's a public auction. With each buyer seeing the offers of other buyers, none need offer their highest price. Indeed, at auctions, it's not a competition to pay the highest price, it's a competition to see which buyers can buy below their highest price – and by how much.

The stupidity of auctioneers – and the reckless manner in which they destroy the value of homes – can be traced back to one word: "PUBLIC".

To be sold by "Public Auction" means to be UNDERSOLD.

And yet if the auction was a "Private Auction", or what's called a "Silent Auction", buyers would reveal their highest price.

Imagine a public auction about to start. There's a large crowd and the auctioneer is looking resplendent. He explains the auction "conditions". Only this time, he says:

"Ladies and Gentlemen. Our vendors have given us one change today. This is to ensure we don't undersell their home like at most auctions. Instead of you all bidding in public, if you wish to buy this home, you will be allowed one private bid only. That bid is to be written on a piece of paper (provided) and placed in an envelope (also provided). In a few minutes, we will open the envelopes and whoever has the highest bid above the reserve price will own this home. Let's get started."

As all competent negotiators know, the difference between the highest and second-highest bidders in a *private* auction can be hundreds of thousands of dollars. Which is the amount lost in public auctions. Instead of a "little bit" above the second-highest bidder, the sellers get a large bit above the second-highest bidder. They get the best price.

REASON 31

Twisted research

Just as the focus of an auction is on the wrong price, so is the focus of the research results.

Each week, agents release stories of how much homes sold *above* the lowest price sellers were willing to accept. It makes auctions seem so enticing. But it's a half-truth.

Headlines say such things as: "Home sells for $2 million above reserve."

As industry observers know, when a home sells far above its reserve, it reveals the ignorance of the agents. It's not the skill of an agent that causes a home to be sold above its reserve, it's because the reserve was too low. Agents often underestimate the value of a home. This is why so many homes are undersold at auctions, especially in a boom.

When the bidding stops, agents swoop on the sellers and say, "This is the best price you are going to get. You should take it. This is what the market is saying."

The sellers should reply: "This is not the best price; it's just the highest bid. Go and do what any good negotiator will do: Discover the buyers' best price."

If auction results were measured by the amounts sold *below* the buyers' best price, instead of amounts above the sellers' lowest price, the truth would be revealed: Thousands of homes undersold every month by tens or hundreds of thousands of dollars.

With the truth revealed, no sellers would ever auction a home again.

REASON 32

Three major prices

At all auctions, there are three major prices. But one price, the most important one for sellers, is not only hidden, it is ignored.

Those three prices are:

1. The **Reserve** Price – the lowest price the sellers are prepared to accept.
2. The **Selling** Price – the price at which the property sold.
3. The **BHP** – the price the buyers were willing and prepared to pay.

How can agents keep getting away with saying auction is the best way to get the best price, when they ignore the best price buyers are willing to pay?

How can sellers get the best price when agents focus solely on their lowest price?

In June 2021, a Brisbane agent's comment made headline news:

"If you don't go to auction in the current market, you're a lunatic."

The newspapers and the major websites – who love auctions because sellers waste massive amounts of advertising money – lapped up the "lunatic" comment[20].

The opposite was the truth: Sellers who auction their homes – especially in a boom – could be classed as lunatics.

The agent who made this comment did what all such agents do – pointed to homes, one in particular, that sold "$1 million above reserve". Of course, no one knows if the buyer of that home was prepared to pay *another million*. And so, the public get fooled into thinking that a home which was *undersold* by $1 million sold for $1 million *extra*.

It's a gigantic cover-up that fools tens of thousands of Australia's home-sellers.

REASON 33

The transparency trap

Transparency – it's a feel-good word. It makes us think we are told the truth and we can see what's going on. With auctions, this is more twisted nonsense. The transparency in auctions does not determine the value of a property; it severely damages the value.

The agent who said sellers would be "lunatics" not to sell by auction, also said: "Auction is the most transparent way of determining the value of a property in this heated market[21]."

Transparent for sellers, sure – all of whom reveal their lowest price. But buyers do not reveal their highest price. That's transparency for sellers, concealment for buyers.

While buyers conceal their highest price, they openly make bids – and this is what agents call "transparent". That's not an advantage to sellers. It might be transparent, but it causes properties to be undersold.

As repeatedly stated, by seeing all other bids, each bidder just makes one bid more than the bidder below them. Buyers conceal their highest price and take full advantage of the one-sided transparency of sellers being forced to reveal their lowest price.

This breaks a basic rule of negotiation: Sellers should never disclose the amount offered by other buyers.

If this sort of "transparency" happened in government tenders, some participants, especially the organisers, would end up in jail.

With auctions, agents push the word "transparent" like it's an advantage. Once again, it's a half-truth. Sellers are forced to be "transparent" by revealing their lowest price. But buyers never have to reveal their highest price.

By making one rule for sellers only, buyers have a huge advantage with auctions. Like cheating exam students, they see what's going on. But sellers are in the dark; they have no idea of the buyers' best prices.

And, of course, this is why their homes are undersold.

If there is one major rule for sellers, the same rule should also apply to buyers.

But not at auctions.

At auctions, transparency is a half-truth, a one-way trap to underselling a home.

"Transparent" might be a feel-good word. But a better word is "fairness".

There's nothing fair about giving buyers a massive advantage and forcing sellers – for whom agents are acting – to accept a major disadvantage.

REASON 34

On-line auctions - the truth on display

With more auctions going on-line, the absurd claims of transparency, the unfairness to sellers, and the brazen best-price lie are on full display.

It's easy to get seduced by the sophistry. Thousands of sellers are lured to losses by on-line auction companies. Especially seemingly respectable companies – one of which recently listed on the stock exchange – erroneously telling sellers, "You'll get the best possible price[22]."

Sellers may think: Surely such companies wouldn't mislead us? If they say their method gets "the best possible price for sellers", it must do so. But no. Not even close.

For decades, auction agents have spun the lie about auctions and the best price. They repeat it automatically with no fear of being taken to task. Incredibly, this lie is repeated throughout the prospectus of the listed on-line auction company. The Chairperson's letter says their method "ensures price maximisation for the seller [23]".

Whether an auction is on-site or on-line, it cannot get the best price if buyers never reveal their best price. As with on-site auctions, sellers disclose their lowest price at on-line auctions, but this transparency only applies to sellers. Buyers do not disclose their highest price which is at odds with the claim "completely transparent sales process". At best, it's *partial* transparency. Again, great for buyers, terrible for sellers.

To be sure, on-line auctions do have some advantages over on-site auctions – such as allowing terms and enabling buyers to bid off-site – but they still can't get the best price. To claim such is to greatly mislead home-sellers who pay dearly for the on-line service.

A public auction is a public auction, no matter how it's promoted.

REASON 35

Three costs instead of one!

When you sell your home, there should be only one cost – commission. That's what happens in most countries. Agents charge one fee to sellers – commission.

Indeed, with ethical businesses, no costs apply until their service is rendered and clients are happy. In real estate, there is a Golden Rule for sellers: *Never pay any money for any reason to any agent until your home is sold and you are happy with the price and service.*

With auctions, it's impossible to apply this rule.

With auctions, sellers have three expenses, all of which are excessive and two are needless.

The first charge is commission. Commission rates are always negotiable. You should negotiate the commission when the agent finds a buyer not when you sign up. This gives agents an incentive to get the best result. But try negotiating the commission with an agent at an auction as the auctioneer is screaming, "Going once, going twice!"

With auctions, the second expense is needless advertising costs. Behind-the-scenes, advertising is a joke with agents. Most agents have buyers on their database.

Your final needless cost with auctions is the amount your home is undersold. This often equals at least 10% of the selling price.

On a $2 million sale price, these three "true costs" usually exceed $230,000[24].

That's the equivalent of paying a commission rate of 11.5%.

Auction is the most expensive way to sell a home.

REASON 36

The "skin-in-the-game" bluff

"Skin-in-the-game": it's a crude expression and when uttered by agents, it reeks of disrespect, even contempt. Again, if sellers could hear how agents use this expression, they'd reject any agents who demand any money before their homes are sold.

All over the world sellers pay nothing until their homes are sold. Advertising is included in the commission. Except in Australia. Most of the world's agents aren't as greedy as Australia's agents who want sellers to have – that skin-crawling expression – "skin in the game".

By investing nothing, and transferring all risk to sellers, agents perpetrate a scam that's shamefully unique to Australia.

The scam is called VPA – Vendor Pays Advertising.

Ethical agents know that VPA is a scam. Sellers can and should refuse to pay it, especially up front. Stand your ground. Find an ethical agent who does not require "skin-in-the-game". Turn it back. Say: "If you want to sell my home, you put skin-in-the-game, just as every ethical agent and agents in other countries do."

Why should Australian sellers be so disadvantaged?

If commission of $30,000[25] is not enough to cover "extras", the agent is either greedy or stupid. Maybe both.

You are putting your greatest asset, your family home, "in the game".

If that's not enough for the agent, find another agent.

REASON 37

Lazy agents

Hard work is anathema to most agents. Other than fake feedback to "condition" sellers to lower their price, sellers rarely see the agent who persuaded them to sign up.

Anyone who calculates the hours of actual work done by an agent (after sellers have signed up for auction) will discover the truth: Almost nothing is done. It's a sit-back-and-wait process. And agents know it. In a 2021 course on how to use an on-line auction system, the trainer admitted this system suited lazy agents[26].

"Incidentals", such as booking needless advertising and other "extras", are handled by junior staff. Then come "open inspections". Each week, an agent "opens" a home for 30 minutes (out of 10,080 minutes per week), supposedly so buyers can "view" the home.

But the big question agents ask at each "open house" is: "Do you have a property to sell?"

It's not uncommon for agents to find three or four sellers – which means another three or four sales – from each auction "marketing campaign".

When sellers see the amount of space given to the agent's name (or photo) and they start to give serious thought to the process, they often get a sinking feeling common to all scam victims – *this is more about them (the agent) than about us (the sellers).*

Agents tell sellers that auctions get the best result. They don't tell sellers what they tell each other – auctions suit lazy agents.

REASON 38

A lead-generation machine

A major reason agents push auctions is because:

"Auctions are a publicity and lead-generation machine for agents."

Five real reasons agents push auctions:

CONTROL. From the minute sellers sign up, they relinquish all control to agents. Signed-up sellers are dubbed "controlled listings". No home-sellers have less control than auction-sellers. Still, with help, they can escape. To cancel an auction, call 1800 1800 18 (no cost or obligation).

FREE PUBLICITY. Agents are obsessed with "profile". With auctions, sellers unwittingly pay to raise the agents' profile. Agents tell sellers that the more ads, the more chance of a higher price – when the opposite is more true. The Real Estate Institute teaches agents: "The more ads with your name on them the more successful you will look." Large numbers of auctions mean large amounts of advertising which creates the impression that an agent is the best. Often, agents already have buyers for a home, yet they waste every cent of the sellers' money to generate maximum publicity for themselves. Plus, many agents get kickbacks from advertisers. The more sellers spend, the more the agents pocket. Conflict of interest? Unethical? Maybe. Read the fine print; it's all there.

MORE LISTINGS. The more enquiry, the more sellers are attracted to the agent. Agents are often trained <u>not</u> to sell homes at open houses as this cuts their supply of leads. One trainer taught: "The worst thing to do [at an 'open home'] is sell the home[27]."

Another said, "A mistake that agents make is the minute there's any excitement around a listing they sell it at the first open. But what you need to do is focus on maximising the number of opens[28]."

BEST PRICE ILLUSION. Because auctions start low, agents say, "Look how the price keeps going up and up. Every bid is more money for the sellers." If a home sells above reserve, it creates the illusion that sellers get the best price. In most cases, the final price is below the buyers' best price. Things move fast which prevents inexperienced and naïve sellers from understanding what's really happening. Homes are massively undersold.

HIGH PRESSURE. Agents enjoy the high pressure ("crunch") at auctions when the bidding stops below the reserve. Intimidation, embarrassment, manipulation, fear tactics – it's all there. Anything to cause sellers to "crack" without time to think.

As one Real Estate Institute training manual teaches agents:

> *"Move quickly,*
> *they are usually numb;*
> *don't give them time to*
> *dwell on the price*[29]*."*

REASON 39

The stimulate scam

Of all auction tricks, the most deadly is the stimulate trick.

It is a favourite with dodgy agents, and it happens before sellers realise what's been done.

Here's how it works: At auctions, bidding often stops well below the reserve. Agents then say to the sellers, "Some bidders won't bid until we are on the market. They're waiting. We don't want to lose them. If you put it on the market, this can stimulate the bidding and the price can really take off."

But what if the sellers put their home on the market to "stimulate" the bidding, and nothing happens? The answer is simple: Their home is sold well below their original reserve price. They have been caught in a common auction con.

Say the reserve is $1.5 million and bids stop at $1.25 million. Under huge pressure from the agent to "stimulate the bidding", sellers "crack".

The agent yells, "It's on the market!" The next word sellers hear is "SOLD!" followed by clapping led by the agents. Their home sells below their original reserve. In this case, a quarter of a million dollars below.

Sellers caught by this scam are emotional wrecks.

In theory, the reserve price protects sellers. In practice, nothing protects sellers when agents use the stimulate scam. As agents are taught at auction training: "The pressure on them is intense and your persistency will win out in the end[30]."

At auctions, "persistency" means high-pressure bullying.

REASON 40

It's a massive bluff

The fall of the hammer means nothing. Yes – nothing.

It's all part of the massive bluff, an intimidation game called "real estate auctions".

Think about it. When is a hammer "legal" for any payment? When you ask for the bill at a restaurant, does the waiter hand you a hammer and say, "Please whack here"?

Are you married? Did a priest or celebrant say, "On the fall of the hammer you are man and wife"? Hardly. At law, you must sign documents before being legally bound. Yes, S-I-G-N.

When an auctioneer yells "SOLD", the sellers or the buyers can yell back, "FORGET IT!". And walk away. Or run if they want to make it fun. Or have mates in a car idling at the kerb. Leap in the back and yell, "GO!" Burn rubber and take off.

Don't believe it? Then go to any auction. Pick an expensive suburb. Agents are too stupid or lazy to "qualify" the buyers. Bid as much as you feel like – all with a smile. Say the final bid is $10 million. If it's you, wait until everyone's gone. Then say to the agent, "Sorry, mate, I've got no money."

What will they do? Nothing. It happens often. Even on the TV show The Block. The winner of the 2020 season just walked away[31]. What happened? Nothing. Auctions are a gigantic bluff. A game of intimidation and bullying based on deception.

APPEAL: Auction sellers suffer enough, so don't deliberately make things worse by ruining their sale. But, if you have been bullied or deceived and you hear "SOLD!" and you are not happy, remember three words – ***DON'T SIGN ANYTHING!*** Then call your solicitor.

Or call Jenman Support on 1800 1800 18 (for support not legal advice).

REASON 41

Independent experts agree - auctions **undersell** homes!

Everyone – other than agents and those who profit from property advertising – who does research into the public auction system agrees: **Auctions undersell homes.**

Independent experts are shocked at how the industry promotes the lie that auctions get the best prices. Anyone who studies the twisted logic soon realises that selling by auction is disastrous.

Geoff Owen is a successful businessperson who lives in one of Sydney's most beautiful suburbs – Darling Point. Geoff is an avid real estate observer, but with a difference. He does not instantly accept claims by agents. Especially with auctions. Geoff writes: "Everything you say about the folly of auctions makes perfect sense to me – and has proven to be correct when we bought at auction (and would have paid more) and sold by Expressions of Interest (and achieved more than we could have achieved at auction)."

One of Australia's dynamic chartered accountants agrees. Having bought a home at auction well below his best price, Paul Siderovski said: "I would never sell a house at auction after knowing what happened and how I paid $200,000 less than I was prepared to pay." As an accountant, Paul has a duty to be responsible with financial figures. Warning home-sellers against selling by auction is not something he takes lightly.

But not only is it his professional opinion, it's a mathematical fact: At auctions, sellers are near certain to undersell their homes. They have almost no chance of getting the highest price.

REASON 42

The 3 "highs" of selling; how sellers are fooled into ignoring the highest price

Just as a magician fools an audience by deflecting attention, so does an auctioneer. Auctions depend on illusions.

Two illusions the auctioneer and his acolyte-agents create are: first, that auctions mean high prices for sellers and, second, that auctions get the *highest* price for sellers.

The first illusion is correct. High prices *can* be achieved at auction. But not, as agents want you to believe, because of an auction. High prices are achieved because buyers like a home.

The second illusion is false. Auctions do *not* assure sellers of the highest price.

There are three HIGHS with selling a home.

1. A HIGH PRICE.
2. A HIGHER PRICE.
3. THE HIGHEST PRICE.

At auction, sellers often get a high price. They may get a higher price than expected – especially in a boom. But the one price they are *not* getting – despite what agents tell them – is the *highest* price.

The highest price is the BEST price.

If you are selling your home, use a method that gets you the best price.

Not public auctions.

REASON 43

Auction truth is banned!

Peter Fox was a detective with the New South Wales Police. In 2012, he became a hero for supporting victims of abuse in the Catholic Church. In 2019, after he retired, Peter wrote a book, *Walking Towards Thunder*.

His opening words were:

"When a person speaks out from within an institution against that institution, they know reprisals are coming. Institutions carry it in their DNA, in-built self-protection, if you like."

I know what Peter means. Reprisals happened to me. And to others who "dare" reveal the truth about real estate, especially with auctions.

Louis Christopher is the most honest real estate researcher in Australia. Before he formed his own company, SQM Research, Louis worked with a research company owned by a media company (Fairfax). Sick of seeing fake auction results, he spoke out. He revealed the truth. He lost his job[32]. In hindsight, it was his best career move. He now works with an honest company – his own – and is widely respected as an honest and accurate property forecaster. One who can't be bought. There is nothing corrupt about Louis Christopher.

When I wrote my first book, *Real Estate Mistakes* in 2000, the public loved it. But most agents loathed it. So fierce was their condemnation, they lobbied the major newspaper groups – Fairfax and News Limited. My book and name were banned from being mentioned in hundreds of local newspapers in Australia.

There is rarely anything negative about auctions in print or on-line media. Truth is shut down. By order of the media's major sponsor, the real estate industry.

REASON 44

Auctions mean **less** buyers

People who do objective research into auctions are astonished at how many half-truths, lies and disadvantages are claimed as advantages.

Nowhere is this more obvious than the claim that "An auction gets you more buyers". This is not even close to true. There are *less* buyers at auctions than normal sales. Often far less.

Auctions repel buyers, many of whom are the best-paying buyers.

Surveys consistently show that more than 90% of buyers despise auctions[33].

All agents hear buyers say: "We are not interested in anything for auction." As one mortgage broker tweeted, "When I see sellers putting their homes for auction, I want to scream: 'You just turned away more than half the buyers.'"

The only buyers who like auctions are those who know that auctions enable them to buy well below their best price.

Investors and bargain-hunters like auctions because they can buy under-value.

Contrary to what agents claim, selling by auction means less buyers.

And less money for sellers.

REASON 45

The "auction area" farce

In some expensive areas, agents love to tell sellers: "This is an auction area."

The (flawed) logic is: *As everyone seems to auction in this area, you should too.*

But beware.

Agents have spent years creating the illusion that auctions are best in these areas. They won't comply easily if you reject a sale by auction. They will put enormous pressure on you to do what they want you to do.

Some agents say, "But how can we find a buyer and sell it if we don't auction?" Agents who make such absurd remarks should be dropped from consideration immediately.

Some agents claim that if you don't use auction, "Buyers think something is wrong." That's a pathetic excuse far removed from the truth. In so-called "auction areas", sellers get a huge advantage by putting their home for normal sale.

Buyers are delighted to see a home they can buy now.

Sellers who "defy the trend" in auction areas and refuse to auction can get a much better result.

When agents say "This is an auction area" they mean an area where sellers are easily duped into auction.

REASON 46

Twice as hard to get a great price

If you want to get agents thinking (about giving up auctions), make this comment: "With auctions you need two buyers, but you only get paid for one sale. That's not good for you."

The way agents get more buyers at an auction is by making buyers think they can buy cheaply.

But when a crowd of "bargain-hunters" turn up at an auction, all expecting to buy the home well under its value, here's what happens: The bidding stops short of its true value.

The agents say: "This is what the market is saying! You must drop your reserve to 'meet the market'."

Under stress, most sellers never realise: The agent has attracted the *wrong* market.

If you want to sell for a high price, you need buyers who can pay a high price. A crowd of bargain-hunters gives agents justification to pressure you to sell cheaply.

The agents get a big commission, but you get a low price.

In normal market conditions (most of the time), it's hard enough to find one buyer willing to pay a great price.

Don't make it twice as hard by selling at auction.

REASON 47

The "happy" justification

To agents, it doesn't matter if sellers don't get the best deal, if *they don't know they didn't get the best deal.*

The typical agent logic is: If sellers are happy, what's the problem? That's like a cheating spouse saying, "As long as my partner doesn't know, there's no problem."

The homes of unknowing "happy clients" are undersold by hundreds of thousands of dollars, all because their agent did not learn how to negotiate.

And yet all agents call themselves "negotiators"; but toddlers are better negotiators. A recent survey of 100 agents showed that none had read a book about negotiation[34].

The common industry attitude is: What does it matter if buyers are willing to pay more – even hundreds of thousands of dollars (or millions!) more? Agents say that's the auction system – and there's nothing they can do. If sellers are happy with the price, they don't need to know they could have got a better price.

Well, the first part is right – underselling of homes is the auction system; but the second part is negligence caused by chronic laziness. Plenty can be done to get the best price for sellers.

Such as stop being so stupid as to use the public auction system.

And instead, learn how to negotiate.

REASON 48

The "flip side" to "success stories"

Every auction agent has great stories of homes selling "well above reserve price". But these "success examples" – as good as they sound – still mean buyers did not pay their highest prices.

Yes, agents are like magicians – keeping the sellers' focus *off* the buyers' highest prices. It's as if agents wave a magic wand and say: "Mr and Mrs Seller, those owners wanted $1.2 million. At auction, bidders pushed the price to $1.7 million. The sellers were delighted. That's $500,000 above reserve!" Clear message: *This could happen to you.*

But there's a flip side to success stories. Never mind the price buyers paid – *how much were they willing to pay?* In this case, the buyers paid $1.7 million, but were willing to pay $2.1 million.

Sure, the home sold $500,000 above reserve, but it also sold *$400,000 below BHP!* The flip side to auction success stories is that they are failure stories. But that truth is hidden.

Here is what to say to agents who brag about auction success stories: "Okay, the property sold half a million dollars above its reserve – which is the sellers' lowest price, right?"

The agent will say, "Yes, that's right."

You then ask: "How much **more** was the buyer prepared to pay?"

Most agents will say they don't know.

You then reply, "So, if the buyer was willing to pay another $400,000, the home could have sold for $900,000 above reserve?" The agent will have to agree. It's auction checkmate.

Your final comment is then: "So, the home you are boasting about having sold for $500,000 above reserve, could have been **undersold** by $400,000?"

REASON 49

Sellers financially sacrificed to improve agents' fake image

Some agents deliberately undersell homes because it's in *their* best interests to do so. They prevent homes from being sold before auction, especially homes that are known as "sure-sellers". By forcing these homes to go to auction, rather than being sold before auction, agents can boast a huge auction "success rate". They make statements such as: "95% of our auctions successfully sell under the hammer."

When agents talk about auctions being "successful", they mean "sold" regardless of price. If owners are conditioned to lower their reserve and pressured to sell for less than they were expecting, it may be a financial disaster for the sellers. But, to agents, these sales are labelled a "success". "Success" to agents means a commission; it's that crass.

For these agents, success is never measured by the happiness of the client or, heaven forbid, whether a home sold for the best price. If those two criteria – happiness and best price – were how auction success was rated, the auction success rate would be close to zero.

Ironically, although auction is the worst way to sell a home, negotiating *before* an auction can be the best way for sellers to get the best price.

Most buyers – especially those who are most keen – want to buy before the auction. But to boost their "auction image", agents tell sellers not to sell before auction. This is terrible advice for sellers because it deprives them of a great chance of getting the best price. To insist that a property be sold at auction is good for agents because it increases their mythological "success rate".

In July 2021, the boss of Australia's largest real estate network listed his home for auction. A week prior to the auction he did what his agents constantly tell sellers *not* to do: he sold *before* the auction[35]. By all reports, he made the smart move and appeared to have sold for the highest price, something that would have been unlikely had he waited for the auction.

A skilled negotiator obtains each buyer's highest price in two ways. First, by telling all buyers that they have one chance to make one offer and, second, by telling them that their offer will not be revealed to other buyers. This cannot be done at a public auction.

If sellers consider selling before auction, agents often say: "We recommend you go to auction." Some also say: "If buyers offer you a price now, they will pay this price at auction. Or more." This is negligent advice from agents who are too stupid to understand maths or too dishonest because their agenda is to be seen as "successful auction sellers".

Thousands of buyers buy homes at auction *below* the prices they offered before the auction or, worse, amounts they were prevented from offering before the auction.

For example: A buyer offers $1.7 million before an auction. The offer is rejected (or suppressed). At the auction, the home sells to the *same* buyer for $1.5 million. This is a common example.

Here's the point sellers are not told: If you get an offer before an auction and you reject it, then, to get the same offer (or better) at the auction, you need other buyers to push that buyer up to (or above) the offered amount. If those buyers are not there – as often happens – or they stay below the offer made before the auction, the sellers lose. Often massively.

The agents then boast: "95% of our properties sell at auction."

Sellers are financially sacrificed so that agents can make spurious "success" claims.

REASON 50

Agents say not getting BHP is not really a "loss"

Agents, many of whom are not financially successful (despite their cars), are quick to claim that underselling at auction is not "technically" a loss.

If the sellers sold their home for, say, a million dollars more than they originally paid, this is a profit of one million dollars.

For example, they bought for $500,000, and sold 20 years later for $1.5 million.

That's not a loss. That's a profit. And a good profit too – a cool million dollars.

And further, agents will claim that if the sellers were expecting, say, $1.3 million, and they got $1.5 million at the auction this means...

Not only did they get $1 million profit,
but they also got $200,000 EXTRA.

All of the above statements are true. Sort of.

Auction agents are notorious for half-truths. That's how they persuade sellers.

Consider this explanation of the difference between a *half-truth* and a whole-truth.

- The price at which a property sells can be called a *half-truth.*
- The price that the buyer who bought that property was *prepared to pay* can be called a whole-truth. That's the **BHP** (Buyers' Highest Price).

If a home can be sold for $2 million yet sells for $1.5 million, the sellers <u>did not get the BHP</u>.

They got $500,000 below the BHP.

If you don't get something you should have got (with a better agent), that's a loss.

The difference between the whole-truth of $2 million and the half-truth of $1.5 million is half a million dollars. The agents may not see that as a loss, but it's not their money.

The only price you want when you sell – by any method – is the BHP. At an auction, unlike other methods, you cannot be assured of getting the BHP.

And if you can't get the BHP, you have lost money. That's the truth.

Never sell by auction.

Always sell by a method that gets you the BHP (Buyers' Highest Price).

REASON 51

The betrayal hurts most

If sellers discover what the agent has been doing to do them with the auction system, it's surprising that what upsets them most is not what you may expect.

They are not hurt about not getting the best price. A bit frustrated, perhaps. Some say it's hard to be perfect. They are not upset that hordes of strangers – most with no intention (let alone ability) of buying – traipsed through their home, stickybeaking in cupboards or drawers. They don't object to the agent using their home as a source of leads.

What makes sellers incandescent with rage is the planned betrayal. The deceit and disloyalty. They were set up from the start – as patsies. They hired a traitor. A sneaky back-stabber whose plan was always to betray them.

And what tipped them off? The conditioning processes. The deliberate emotional and psychological pain of those pre-planned "conditioning letters", the set format of "regular feedback" – all part of the betrayal.

Like all of us, sellers are human. They forgive mistakes. They forgive incompetence. They don't like it, but they forgive sloppiness, bad manners, even discourtesy.

But they never forgive the deliberate pre-arranged betrayal of the auction conditioning system.

Damage to the value of our home, okay. But damage to our feelings, betraying the trust we placed in you, that's not okay. It's dastardly disloyal. Such betrayal is unforgivable.

If you auction your home, you invite the worst level of betrayal to descend upon you. But that's the auction system.

REASON 52

Auction agents are neither honest nor competent. Here's proof.

To get the best price for your home, find the best agent. No matter how long it takes. Better to spend three weeks searching for the right agent than three months stuck with the wrong agent.

The best agents are honest and competent. They are also hard-working. Reject agents who claim that auction is the best way to get the best price. They are neither honest nor competent.

If an agent says, "Auction is the best way to get the best price," please realise that you are likely looking at a fool or a shonk. If you want to give the agent a chance (right of reply), you can ask **4 SIMPLE QUESTIONS to test their honesty and competency.**

You may like to start by saying: "Well, that's good because we want the best price, but we are not sure an auction will do that. May we ask you four questions?"

Q1: When buyers come to the auction, how do you know the best price they will pay?

[If they admit they don't know, that will require another question, such as: *"Well if you don't know the buyers' best price, how can you get us the best price?"*]

Q2: If a buyer is willing to pay us $2 million, would you suggest we accept $1.8 million?

[This is a great test of an agent's competency/honesty. They will surely say no, they would never recommend such a thing. Which leads to your next question: *"If we auction as you suggest, and our reserve is $1.5 million and the highest bid is $1.8 million, you will suggest we sell; but if the buyer who bids $1.8 million can pay $2 million, we'd miss out on $200,000. How do you prevent this? After all, you said, 'auction gets* *the best price' and the best price this buyer will pay is $2 million. An auction would mean you tell us to do what you just said you'd never do, namely, accept an offer $200,000 below what the buyer was willing to pay."*]

Q3: Have you read any books or done any courses on negotiation?

The ability to negotiate the best price is the main skill you need in an agent; yet almost no agents have studied the topic of negotiation. You can ask: *"Do you mind sharing what you learned about negotiation and how it can help us sell for the best price?"* If you are not impressed with the reply, you have not found the right agent.

Q4: You ask us to reveal our lowest price. Do you ask buyers to reveal their highest price?

They will likely say no. Or offer some excuse. In which case you say, *"How can you discover the best price buyers are prepared to pay if you don't ask them?"*

REASON 53

Fake clearance rates

Another common lie about auctions is their purported success rate. Each week, false figures are released about the "success" of auctions. They are called "Auction Clearance Rates".

The real estate industry has one purpose with "Auction Clearance Rates" – to deceive the public, in two ways. The first deception is to make you think the property market is always performing well. The second deception is to make you think auctions are always successful.

"Auction Clearance Rates" are lies. Not some of the time, *all the time.* They are deliberately fudged. If stockbrokers released such fake information, they would likely be jailed.

"Auction Clearance Rates" are laughable. A joke.

Here's an example of what happens each week:

Melbourne: 1369 auctions and 507 sales. Fake clearance rate 63%. Truth 37%.

Sydney: 1049 auctions and 603 sales. Fake clearance rate 77%. Truth 57%[36].

"Auction Clearance Rates" are inflated by about 30% – sometimes double. For a clearance rate of 80%, the truth will be around 50%, maybe less.

One weekend, in Perth, there were 21 auctions held and no sales. The clearance rate was claimed as 30%[37].

Everyone, other than the trusting public, knows what's happening.

The people and the companies that release the clearance rates are paid by agents.

REASON 54

No "right time" or "wrong time"

They say it with such authority – as if they are oracles of property: Agents who announce: "This is an *ideal auction property*."

Translation: *This is easy for me to convince sellers to auction.*

Or, they say: "This is an ideal **time** to auction." Followed by: "In this market, with so many buyers around, you'd be mad not to auction."

Translation: *In a boom, it's easier to convince sellers to auction.*

It's quite understandable how you can be drawn in. Agents are "experts". They are supposed to know. Why would they give the wrong advice?

Always remember, there are only TWO REASONS agents give wrong advice about auctions:

INCOMPETENCY OR **DISHONESTY**

But incompetent, or dishonest, does not mean unconvincing.

Fools can appear smart. Incompetent agents may appear competent. Some even believe auction is the best way to sell; this makes them more convincing. Passion persuades.

But auction is never the best way to sell a home. And anyone who claims such is either incompetent or dishonest.

No matter what the market conditions; no matter how "unique" your home, no time is a good time to undersell your home.

No home is ever the "right home" to be undersold.

No time is ever the "right time" to be undersold.

REASON 55

Weather, traffic, alarm clocks

Bob Hartford slept in. The alarm didn't go off. And his wife didn't wake him; she thought the auction was in the afternoon. But no, it's scheduled for 11 in the morning. It's now four minutes to 11 am. They are stuck in Saturday traffic five kilometres from the home being auctioned. When he first saw it, three weeks ago, Bob loved this home. It's his dream home. The agents quoted "around $1.8 million". Bob will go to $2.5 million. He must have it.

But now, all seems lost.

Frantically, he calls the agent. It goes to voicemail. He swears. How can agents be so stupid? He's got $2.5 million to spend and they don't answer.

Bob tries to think. Nothing.

If only someone could get there and stall the auction. He can't think of anyone.

Bob Hartford, successful executive, father of four, hard-working, honest, is near tears. This is the home he's always wanted. He is sure he can out-bid any buyer, but not in traffic. Darned auctions.

He tried to make an offer before auction, but the agent said no.

When he arrives, the SOLD sign is up.

Gutted, Bob asks: "How much did it sell for?"

"$2.1 million," says the grinning agent. "A hundred thousand above reserve. Great result."

"Great result, be damned," Bob muttered to himself. "The sellers lost $400,000. I lost a home I loved."

Maybe Bob can offer the buyers some (or all!) of the extra money he was ready to pay – if they drop out and let him be the buyer.

It happens many times – late bidders offer winning bidders money to walk away. Of course, the sellers still lose a few hundred thousand dollars.

Another massive hidden auction loss. This time due to the stupidity of a deadline.

A deadline that puts buyers at the mercy of alarm clocks, traffic, weather, or so many other reasons that can cause them to be late.

And cause sellers to lose a few hundred thousand dollars[38].

REASON 56

Agents always win with auctions

When Robin was selling her late father's home on Sydney's Lower North Shore, she took time to understand how real estate operates. Like anyone who does such research, Robin was horrified at the deception endemic amongst agents. But what really outraged her was how agents transfer all risk to home-sellers.

As Robin said, "All business involves risk. As a consultant, there are risks in my business." That's the way of business. You accept risks, you reap rewards. Unlike agents, who transfer risk to their clients thereby making sure that, no matter what, agents can't lose. Only sellers and buyers can lose. Especially at auctions. No matter what the result at auctions, agents win.

If the home sells, the agents win.

If the home does not sell, the agents still win by getting extra listing leads many of which become sales with big commissions. Plus, agents get free advertising. Many get kickbacks ("rebates") from money they persuaded sellers to pay for needless services and benefits, the worst of which is the massive amount wasted on needless advertising.

Unlike sales by private treaty – or other methods more beneficial to sellers – where agents may be out-of-pocket, with auctions agents have zero risk.

With auctions, only sellers and buyers can lose. By transferring all risk to the sellers and buyers, agents can't lose, no matter what.

And that's just another reason agents push auctions.

Nothing to do with getting the best price for the home-sellers.

REASON 57

True success rate is almost non-existent for sellers

Although most never know it, sellers almost always lose when they sell by auction.

If their home sells at the auction, it's likely to have been undersold. After all, are sellers supposed to believe the result of all auctions is a coincidence where the highest price paid by the highest bidder is an exact match for the highest the bidder was willing to pay?

If their home does not sell at auction, sellers lose thousands of dollars in advertising costs – from which agents profit handsomely.

With auctions, agents profit from the losses of sellers.

If a home does not sell, its value is damaged, often severely. It becomes an "auction lemon".

Once a home fails to sell at auction, the pressure on owners increases. Agents prey on this pressure. The message to the sellers is: "If you think the price now is low, wait a few weeks. You'll wish you had taken the price being offered now."

Most agents have a "continuing agency clause" in their auction agreements. This means that even when sellers are unhappy, even if they have been the brunt of false quoting, constant conditioning, and weeks of pressure, they are stuck with this agent.

Agents can't lose at auctions. That's why agents push auctions.

Sellers can't win at auctions. That's why sellers must reject auctions.

REASON 58

Consumers lose at every auction

In speeches I have made to the real estate industry, I constantly stress that my aim is not to hurt agents, it's to protect consumers, especially those drawn into the auction system. A statement I often make is this: "If protecting consumers means agents are hurt, it must follow that agents are hurting consumers."

When I make that statement, agents shake their heads in disagreement. I then say that all ethical companies offer customers something agents seldom offer: GUARANTEES.

I say to agents: "If you believe sellers and buyers do not get hurt at auctions, why don't you offer a guarantee? The guarantee can state that if they lose any money, you will refund their losses – such as when losing bidders lose a couple of thousand dollars on reports and legal costs. And then, if the sellers' homes do not sell, you agree to refund the advertising costs – because, after all, you profited from the advertising. But if the property sells you do not have to refund advertising costs. And if the house sells for less than the highest price the buyers were prepared to pay, you do not have to refund the sellers' actual loss (which may be hundreds of thousands of dollars), but you will forfeit your commission. How does that sound?"

Their answer – shouted by many agents – is: "That means we'd lose at every auction!"

I ask them to think about what they just said.

If agents had to guarantee auctions, agents would lose at every auction.

So, who's losing at every auction now?

REASON 59

If you check both sides, you'd never sell by auction

There's an old bush saying: "No matter how thin you slice the pancake, there are always two sides." When you think of selling your home, you're likely to do what most sellers do: Invite a few agents to your home and ask two questions: *How much can you sell my house for?* And: *How much will you charge me?*

By the time you meet your third agent, you'll feel you're speaking to the same person each time, but in different clothes. They all say the same things. They all recommend auction.

"This is a lovely home."

"Hard to estimate it's value in this market."

"The best way to get the best price is to take it to auction."

You'll be assailed with reasons why each agent is best. Unless you're careful, you will choose the biggest liar. And that can seriously damage your home's value. But there is something you have not done – and it's something few sellers do. Research. Check the other side of "the pancake". You've heard the reasons why you *should* auction. But you are unaware that all those reasons are, at best half-truths and, at worst, total lies.

You are being "sold".

Think about it: You have met several agents, none of whom you totally trust. So don't do what most sellers do now – and accept the advice of these agents. Check out reasons why you should not auction. Get independent advice, from someone who's not going to earn a commission.

If you check both sides of the auction story, you'll *never* sell by auction.

REASON 60

The popularity myth peer pressure and the dark side

One of the biggest real estate myths is that auctions are "popular". It is agents and their zest to make sales with less effort that leads to an increase in auctions.

There is tremendous peer pressure for agents to push auctions. Franchise networks push offices to do more auctions. Agency managers push salespeople to sign up sellers for auction. The pitch is always: "Auctions are better for us; get more auctions."

Even when agents have personal experience that auctions are wrong, they still push auctions.

Nancy[39] grew up in Indonesia. When she migrated to Australia, she found a unit in the Sydney suburb of Kingsgrove. It was being auctioned. She asked the agent to explain the auction process. The agent said the highest bidder gets to buy the property – provided the highest bid is above the sellers' reserve price.

Nancy wanted to pay $750,000. When she arrived at the auction, she showed the agent her cheque for $75,000, being 10% of her best price.

The auction began with a bid of $650,000. It rose in bids of $10,000 each. When the bidding reached $680,000 the auctioneer yelled, "It's on the market, going to be sold."

The bids slowed to $5000 amounts and then, when it hit $700,000, it stopped. Silence. The auctioneer said, "Can I see another thousand dollars anywhere?" Nancy raised her hand. The auctioneer yelled, "Seven hundred and one thousand dollars. Thank you, madam."

A few seconds later someone else bid $702,000. The auctioneer asked Nancy if she wanted to bid again. She nodded and the auctioneer yelled: "The bid is with you at seven hundred and three thousand dollars. Any more bids? For the first time. For the second time. For the third and final time, it's going to be sold."

He pointed to Nancy. "Sold to you at $703,000!"

Nancy was in shock. She had told the agent she wanted to pay $750,000. She had shown him her cheque for $75,000. And yet, she bought the apartment for $703,000, a whopping $47,000 below her highest price. She didn't even ask for a discount.

The owners were smiling; they got $23,000 above their "reserve" of $680,000. "I felt sorry for them," Nancy said. "They missed out on $43,000."

Today Nancy works in real estate. And yes, she often suggests homeowners sell by auction. As she is expected to do.

And then there's Stephen[40].

When he started in real estate, Stephen was determined to do the right thing. He worked in an office where the manager supported his ethical desire.

But now Stephen works in a franchised office. He's instructed to push auctions. He asks all sellers to fork out $5000 in non-refundable advertising costs.

Stephen has crossed to the "dark side". And he knows it. He told me that for sellers who come to him "from Jenman", he'd agree to "treat them ethically".

I thanked him. But then I said, "Stephen, why don't you treat all your sellers ethically like when you started in real estate?"

It's called peer pressure. In real estate, agents do what their colleagues expect them to do – and that's whatever's best for agents not sellers.

As Michael Kies, Australia's best real estate trainer, explains: "Today's agents are addicted to placing their own interests first."

REASON 61

The three-stages lie

Auction agents are obsessed with the image of auctions. No matter what happens, agents say "This is how it's meant to be". There is no such thing as failure.

It's not just "clearance rates"; the whole system is a façade. If sellers question anything or raise obvious points, agents respond with a slick line from their auction playbook. Convoluted and nonsensical verbiage to hide the truth.

Many sellers throw their hands in the air over the agent's constant self-serving spin. Having signed up, they go along. But they are thinking: "This doesn't make sense."

Agents refuse to concede there is anything wrong with their precious auction system. Whatever happens, they say it is "meant to happen" (*"Part of the plan, Mr and Mrs Seller"*).

They use the "Three-Stage-Lie" They tell owners – many of whom, by this stage, are losing all patience with the constant claptrap – that this is "meant to happen". All part of the plan.

"Don't worry," says the agent. "Auction is a three-stage process. You can sell **before** the auction, you can sell **at** the auction, or you can sell **after** the auction. Isn't this good? You get three chances to get the best price for your home."

Yes, and if you believe that, as the saying goes, you'll believe anything.

Cut your losses. Fire the agent. Find a better agent and a better selling system.

REASON 62

Auction lemons

When homes fail to sell at auction their value usually plunges. These publicly rejected homes are "auction lemons".

When an auction fails, buyers have two thoughts.

First: "What's wrong with the home?"

Second: "The sellers want too much." After all, according to agents, auctions get the highest price; so, homes that fail at auction must be overpriced.

Yes, "greedy owners" is a common belief.

When auctions fail, agents, like circling sharks, move in on financially wounded home-sellers. As one auction trainer taught: "You have a vendor with an even greater problem, even higher motivation, and he will take almost any advice you care to give him[41]."

Of course, "almost any advice" means *almost any price.* Bad for sellers, of course. Great for agents. They make a sale.

There is only one way to be sure your home never becomes an auction lemon: Never auction.

REASON 63

Dodgy buyers and the white-ant techniques

The real estate industry can bring out the worst in anyone. Chronic suspicion permeates auctions. It's like a putrid stench. One observer quipped: "Take the third letter in the word 'auction' – C – and move it to the front and it gives you a big hint: CAUTION!"

An atmosphere of distrust does not invoke fair conduct. Rather, it leads to all sorts of nefarious behaviour. Public auctions are ideal arenas for dodgy buyers (and hired buyers' agents) to "white-ant" a property and turn off other buyers. Even honest and well-meaning buyers (and their advocates) feel forced to tell lies to protect themselves or to get a better deal.

One of Australia's well-known buyers' agents[42] openly suggests lying as a strategy. It comes down to fighting lies with lies. "The aim of the game is to win and buy the property for the cheapest possible price," he says.

One method used by this agent – and ruthless buyers – is to approach bidders at auctions and pay them to stop bidding. "Sometimes we'll go to a bidder and offer them large sums of money to stop bidding," this agent reportedly said[43]. A few thousand dollars in cash and some intimidatory words gets rid of competition. Such tactics kill the sellers' chance of a good price.

Some bidders ask questions about alleged negative aspects of a home, creating fear and doubt among other bidders, many of whom then walk away.

Unscrupulous buyers love auctions. They "white-ant" a home and damage its value. Anything to achieve their goal of a low price.

Inexperienced owners and incompetent agents are no match for sharp buyers and their advocates who openly boast about "controlling an auction" and reducing the price[44].

REASON 64

The dirty digital footprint

Just like people, homes have a reputation.

Failed auction campaigns and the evidence on-line can ruin a home's reputation, its appeal and, worst of all, its value. Nothing will erase its digital footprint.

With a public auction, everything is public. Your privacy is gone – for good.

Everything you ever do with your home – or everything that happens – from the time you sign up for an auction is accessible. From the number of days on the market, to the price offered and the home being passed in – and at what price – it's all on display.

If you change agents, all agents are listed. If buyers ask former agents why they did not sell your home, they will blame you or the home. Fired agents denigrate homes. They never blame themselves.

Plastic bottles last up to 450 years. Plastic bags last up to 1000 years. Negative information about your auction lasts forever – certainly your lifetime. Every time you try to sell, every agent with whom you listed, every price at which you tried and failed – it is there for all to see.

Homes that fail at auction are perpetually rejected.

Don't risk your home becoming a reject.

REASON 65

Bigger value, bigger loss

Losses among expensive homes at auction can total millions of dollars.

Auction agents perpetuate a massive con-job on the wealthy. They say, "Expensive homes should be auctioned."

But that's another myth.

All that happens if expensive homes are auctioned is that sellers lose more.

Instead of losing hundreds of thousands of dollars, owners of expensive homes stand to lose two or three million dollars.

Every wealthy person who takes the time to understand auctions soon catches on. They see how auctions undersell homes. They don't need to be told twice.

Many expensive homes have owners who refuse to sell by auction.

The owners of wealthy homes – especially those who acquired their wealth through hard work and prudence – won't let their homes be undersold.

These owners rarely get caught selling by auction.

REASON 66

Developers don't auction!

Property developers are experts. With years of experience, they know the best ways to sell.

Successful property developers don't sell by auction.

Developers are obsessed with getting the maximum price. Their success depends on it.

Developers know that the real estate spin, "Auctions get the best price", is nonsense. Such nonsense fools inexperienced sellers, but not developers.

Property developers understand how auctions get the second-best price and how that can be hundreds of thousands of dollars below the best price.

No developers want to discount their properties by hundreds of thousands of dollars each.

Harry Triguboff of Meriton Properties is Australia's first property billionaire. He is considered the most successful developer in our history.

In more than 60 years, Mr Triguboff has developed and sold thousands of properties. How many has he sold by auction? None.

Why not?

Harry "wants the best price". Auctions do not get the best price.

All property developers, including Australia's most successful developer, often *buy* properties at auction. They don't sell at auction.

Developers reject selling by auction. And so should you.

REASON 67

Most bids are below the best the buyers can pay

For most of an auction, every bidder is bidding well below the price they are willing to pay.

It makes no sense – as far as sellers are concerned. Sellers want high bids, not low bids.

Once these low bids reach the sellers' lowest price, the property soon sells – to bidders who bid less than they were willing to pay.

Sure, sometimes sellers get above their lowest price, but they rarely get the BHP.

The crowds on auction day want to grab a bargain. And, as with most auctions, the winning bidder buys UNDER the price they are willing to pay.

Auctions are potential bargain time for buyers.

So, next time you see any bidder at an auction, remember: They are offering *less* than they are willing to pay. Especially the winning bidder!

Think about that, for your sake.

And insist on selling with a method where buyers must offer their best price.

REASON 68

Appearance and reality

The English writer W Somerset Maugham was renowned for his ability to see through the façades in daily life. His analysis of human nature made him the world's most successful writer in the mid-twentieth century.

Maugham followed an important precept: *Beware of what crowds are doing.* It was this rule that helped him avoid the huge losses in the 1929 stock market crash.

He said: "The fact that a great many people believe something is no guarantee of its truth."

Maugham would have seen straight through real estate auctions.

From an early age, he was an astute observer of people. Like many who succeed, he avoided mistakes by studying the mistakes of others. He looked at people who succeeded and asked *why* they succeeded. And he looked at people who failed and asked the same question. He knew that most people fail financially in life. He reasoned, therefore, that it is usually safe to assume that what most people are doing is wrong.

Maugham was especially cognisant of appearances. He looked beyond the surface, especially when something appeared to be successful but didn't feel right. He trusted his instinct. And his first instinct was to look for the reality behind every appearance.

One of his stories was *Appearance and Reality.*

Had he been selling his home, agents would have created the appearance that auctions get the best price. But the wise writer would have looked behind the façade.

He would have discovered the reality: Auctions are the worst way to sell a home.

There is a huge difference between the appearance and the reality of auctions.

REASON 69

"Quote it low, watch it go!"

It's the mantra of the auction system, a phrase that spells a philosophy of deceit guaranteed to get agents more sales.

Here it is:

"Quote em low, watch em go. Quote em high, watch em die."

Literal translation: *If we give buyers a false low quote, we get the properties sold.*

A false low quote attracts lots of buyers. The more buyers we attract the more we can say to the sellers, "See, this is what the market is saying."

The sellers, whose heads are spinning, cannot deny the evidence: All these buyers and the highest bid is well below what the sellers were expecting.

The agent says, "You can't ignore the market."

The sellers see the buyers and believe this *is* the market. It does not occur to the sellers that the agents – by deliberately quoting low – attracted the wrong market. They are too shocked to realise this point. They want to sell; that's why they chose auction.

Although they were promised a higher price, the agent is saying "this is the market". If they say no, they could be left with no one.

Under pressure, they do what most sellers do when bidding stops at a low price.

They crack. They sell at this low price.

And the agents make another sale thanks to the *"Quote em low, watch em go"* philosophy.

REASON 70

The motive is revealed

Just as you must never reveal your lowest price, you never reveal the *reason* you are selling.

Just as they want to know the sellers' lowest price, auction agents are obsessed with knowing the sellers' motives. Next thing, the sellers' motives are broadcast to the world.

As good negotiators know, if you reveal your motive, you weaken your position. When selling a home, you should negotiate from a position of strength. The auction system is bad enough, as it starts at a low price, but to compound that disadvantage by promoting the reason for sale does nothing except further lower a home's value.

The reason for sale is no one's business other than the sellers'.

Headlines such as "Owner Bought Elsewhere" or "Selling Due to Ill-Health" or "Under Instructions from Mortgagee" all attract bargain-hunters.

Explicit motives attract vultures. Bad enough to sell with a system that creates lower prices. Worse, to attract buyers who want to pay even lower prices.

Sell from strength. Promote the property's great points. List its features and advantages.

Be proud of the home being sold.

Keep your motive personal – and avoid auctions.

REASON 71

Beware of the greed trap

Agents are taught to "push the greed button". Greedy people are easy to persuade (and cheat). But agents are wrong. They assume sellers are as greedy as they are. But it is not greed to want to sell your home for the best price. It's financial prudence.

Agents say, "Buyers are liars", which is better than admitting they can't qualify buyers. They then label sellers with the "greedy" tag.

It would be wrong to say that sellers can't be swayed when quoted a huge price. Pushing the "greed button" gets attention. It's human nature. And "success stories" are tempting. They shut off reason. Sellers want similar stories to be true about their homes.

Enter the greed trap.

Most people worry about money. So, it's not so much greed sellers feel, it's excitement at the prospect of less worry. When agents say auction gets a higher price, sellers fall into their trap.

And here's the chutzpah of agents: Later, when sellers insist on the price quoted by agents, those same agents call *them* greedy.

Don't let agents appeal to your greed. Sure, we are all tempted at times. But let's not step into the greed trap and sell by a method that benefits agents and hurts us. Use common sense.

Here's how to know if agents are trying to find your greed button. Will the agent accept no commission if they can't sell your home at their quoted price – or better? If not, why not?

If you are not greedy, don't fall into the greed trap. Reject auction and get a better price.

And that's not greed – it's doing well for your family.

REASON 72

A man with a hammer

Whatever makes anyone think that a man yelling at buyers with a hammer in his hand makes buyers pay their best price?

At the auction, the auctioneer's black sports car is prominently parked. He struts up and down raising his voice. The grand master in control. He loves it. Endearing stuff, it's not.

Auctioneers yell at buyers in front of strangers. The buyers stand on the curb. Some sit in the gutter. Auction agents don't care about anything other than making a sale at any price.

The thrill of an auction excites them no end, especially when they hear the word "SOLD". They think about the amount of their commission. None calculate (or care) how much a home is undersold. That's not for discussion.

Auction is quintessential "grab-it-and-run" real estate.

If agents studied negotiation, they would never recommend selling by auction – unless they had another motive, such as to sell at any price. It's not their asset; what do they care? High price or low price, it always means a high commission.

But consider this: If agents got no fee unless homes sold at the price they first quoted the sellers, most agents would go broke.

HINT: Many people feel that women make better negotiators than men[45]. Women comprise almost 50% of today's real estate salespeople. Yet, how many female auctioneers do you see? Almost none. When asked why, women agents reply, "Auctions do not suit my style." Women are not as comfortable with deceit and bullying. Auction agents are hopeless negotiators. Women are better negotiators, especially in real estate. Maybe sellers should interview more women agents[46].

REASON 73

The "can't sell a secret" myth

A common line from agents – to make sellers waste money on needless advertising – is to say: "You can't sell a secret."

Again, more nonsense. Again, the opposite is more likely the truth.

Any agent who says, "You can't sell a secret", knows nothing about sales. And they certainly don't understand the principle of making something special – even secretive – which is one of the best ways to influence buyers to pay their best price.

There is plenty of evidence that the less advertising, the higher the price.

When your home is mass advertised, it goes into the "Comparison Pool". Buyers compare your home with others. The homes they are most likely to buy are those at lower prices. To attract these buyers, you must lower your price too. This is what happens when you allow your home to be tossed in among other homes. It's like being in a shopping aisle. Shoppers price-shop and the lowest-priced items win.

Don't play that game.

Buyers often pay more for homes that are *not* advertised.

Warning: Find an agent who's a skilled negotiator. Reject those who claim that "you can't sell a secret".

Smart agents know: Secrets can sell for the best prices.

Nothing secret about auctions.

REASON 74

"Unconditional" is **not** a benefit!

Agents claim that one of the big advantages about auctions is that buyers can't change their minds. The sale is unconditional. But that's not an advantage; it's a disadvantage.

Please think about it.

Making a contract "unconditional" eliminates many buyers. It's insanity. Many buyers need conditions in a contract – often on finance or perhaps selling another home.

"Conditional" is not a bad thing; it's a good thing. It enables sales to happen that would not otherwise have happened. And besides, most (at least 80%) conditional sales proceed.

Sure, buyers can't change their minds at an auction, but neither can sellers. Once an auction ends and the sellers have been psychologically battered down in price and have signed a contract, there's no turning back. It doesn't matter if the sellers endured weeks of pre-planned conditioning and were tricked into lowering their reserve, there is nothing they can do about underselling their home by hundreds of thousands of dollars.

There are two main buying factors in a real estate negotiation – price and *terms*. By agreeing to terms (conditions) requested by buyers, sellers can get a much better price.

To refuse to provide terms to buyers is to shut out most buyers in many areas. And these are often the buyers who will pay the best price.

Auctions create rigidity. But flexibility is what's needed to get the best price.

REASON 75

A flawed system

Although real estate attracts unsavoury types – especially in a boom – not everyone enters real estate intending to be unethical.

Within days, however, eager rookies witness skulduggery all around them. Many are horrified. Sales staff turnover, especially in the first year, can hit 90%. And it's not because those who quit are "losers" (as those who remain label them), it's because people of integrity abhor what they see. They are disgusted at what they are told to do, especially with auctions.

So, although most people in real estate don't start out being dishonest, flawed systems mean dishonesty is inevitable.

Without deceit, auction agents struggle to succeed. One auction trainer said, "Auctions are about fooling people and any of you who deny that, well, you are either a liar or a fool[47]."

With no hope of changing entrenched thinking, ethical people struggle to embrace deception as a career way of life.

Each year, thousands of people quit real estate, disillusioned and emotionally damaged. None forget the excruciating experience. Those who remain learn to embrace wanton ways, mainly for one reason – money.

It's common to hear agents say that the money they earn gives them a better life. They rationalise. But they all know the truth: What they are doing is wrong.

It's impossible to do good in a system as badly flawed as auctions.

REASON 76

Many buyers won't wait!

The agent was fuming. He had 12 homes scheduled for auction at the end of the month. Like many agents, he was doing what his franchise masters instructed – "Push auctions; it increases our brand."

So why was he upset?

"I could have sold all these homes several times over by now if they weren't for auction," he said. "But head office wants everything auctioned because it makes them look successful. And it promotes the network. It's a joke[48]."

This agent was lamenting what all agents know – instead of causing sales, auctions lose sales. Many buyers will not wait weeks to buy a home. If they see a home they like, they want to pay a deposit, sign a contract, and buy now. They don't want to be told no, you must wait.

But that's exactly what happens with homes being auctioned – agents chase buyers away. They tell them to come back in three weeks. What sort of sales system is that?! In the time before the auction, buyers often find other homes available for immediate sale.

The angry agent was right. He was pressured into auctions by his franchise group. He could have sold all these homes long before the auction date. And for better prices.

He also said, "By the time the auction comes, the best buyers have bought elsewhere. The sellers often end up with a lower price at the auction."

Don't chase buyers away. If buyers want to pay their highest price now and sign a contract, let them do it. Make the sale as soon as you find hot buyers. Don't let them go cold.

Don't chase buyers away. Don't auction.

REASON 77

Fear of loss causes avoidance

There is no method of sale that treats buyers as badly as the auction method. Buyers who are treated badly by agents soon become despondent.

As buyers struggle to get a straight answer from agents, and as they keep missing out on homes they love, despondency turns to anger. Then chronic cynicism.

Soon, they say: "All agents are darned liars. Can't believe any of them."

Buyers begin to understand how lies and greed infest real estate; for example, they start to add on about 20% to agents' quotes. If an agent says a home will sell for $1 million, buyers automatically believe the sellers want at least $1.2 million.

It gets to the stage that buyers barely believe anything they're told. And so, they avoid properties that may have been suitable. Especially those being auctioned.

Many times, after a home is sold at auction, buyers will say: "Gee, we'd have paid more but thought we had no chance."

Be straight with buyers and get a better price. You can't be straight with a crooked system such as auctions.

Never auction your home.

REASON 78

Buyers forbidden from increasing offers

Imagine sitting at a table and negotiating a property sale. Imagine buyers making an offer. The sellers are not happy with the offer. So, the buyers increase their offer. This happens in a sensible negotiation. It does not happen at an auction. Indeed, it cannot happen at an auction.

Buyers at an auction must wait their turn to make an offer (place a bid). Even if they want to increase their own offer (bid) the auctioneer will likely say no. Most get puzzled. You can't bid unless it's your turn.

If you have been to an auction, you will have seen the auctioneer point to a person and say, "The bid is with you, Sir/Madam." If Sir/Madam bids again, the auctioneer may admonish them, schoolteacher style: "No, Sir/Madam, I told you, the bid is with you."

Buyers' agents attend auctions constantly – most are stunned at the stupidity, especially when auctioneers refuse to allow buyers to bid "out of turn". If the highest bidder wishes to increase a bid, buyers' agents watch on, laughing at the stupidity of the auctioneer and his agents.

Auctioneers who refuse to allow bidders to increase their bid if they are the most recent bidder might as well yell to the crowd:

"Excuse me, this is an auction. We are forbidden from getting the best price."

All auctioneers should give up auctions, take a course in negotiation and learn how to sit down at a negotiation table. But then they wouldn't have the crowds and the "profile" of auctions. Nor a method of winning listings, conditioning sellers, and "crunching" them to sell under pressure at the auction.

REASON 79

The sticky-beak repellent

One of the best things about a new home is privacy. You get a home no one else knows. You are the first person to use the bathroom, to sleep and snore in the bedroom. It's your home and yours alone. The fact that a home has never been with anyone else is appealing to many buyers.

On the contrary, homes where hordes of strangers and sticky-beaks have wandered through is a huge turn-off for buyers – especially those who value their privacy.

Many buyers refuse to inspect homes that are widely publicised.

Aside from the feel-good personal factor, there's also safety. One of the first questions asked by police officers at a burglary is: "Has this home been for sale recently?" All sorts of people visit homes for sale, including burglars.

Imagine buying a home and having the locals say: "Yes, I've been through that home."

The best-paying buyers will pay a premium to be one of the first (or only) buyers to inspect a home.

Protect your home's value. Protect your privacy. Don't open your home to all and sundry. It might increase the agent's profile, but it will lower your price.

A lower price makes a home easier to sell. It means agents get paid fast.

And that's the purpose of auctions.

REASON 80

Buyers' agents love auctions!

A new "type" of agent has exploded on the Australian real estate scene in the twenty-first century – the buyers' agent. These agents – many of whom are sellers' agents who've "switched sides" – make it harder for sellers to get a good price, especially at auctions.

Buyers now have agents who show them how to "steal a deal" at auctions. If you are selling your home by auction and buyers hire a good buyers' agent, you are in trouble.

Buyers' agents buy homes at auction below the price buyers are willing to pay. These agents and their buyers laugh with delight. They can't believe sellers can be so foolish.

But it's not foolishness; sellers are conned into auctions.

In 1996, my wife and I found our dream land – five acres in Sydney's north-west. Our limit was $902,000. Our buyers' agent bought the land for $700,000. When the agent discovered "Jenman was the buyer", he called the media, saying: "The guy who says auctions get lower prices paid $50,000 above reserve. Ha-ha."

A journalist asked us: "Did you pay $50,000 above the reserve?" We answered: "We didn't know that the sellers' reserve was $650,000. Sure, we paid $700,000, which is $50,000 more than the sellers' lowest price. But we were prepared to pay $902,000. We saved $202,000."

We love auctions – to buy. Never to sell.

Patrick Bright is an experienced buyers' agent. In 2007, he published a book, *The Insider's Guide to Saving Thousands at Auction*. He wrote: "I have bought many properties at what I would consider bargain prices at auctions, considering what they were really worth and the price we were prepared to pay."

As he also says, "Many people believe, and many selling agents will tell you, an auction is the best way to get the best price for your property. It simply isn't true[49]."

When the boss of a real estate network said it was a "myth" that bargains could be found at auctions, another buyers' agent, David Morrell, responded, "This man must have blinkers on." Morrell, who also wrote a book on how buyers save thousands, said buying properties below their value at auction is "similar to stealing ice cream from babies".

Like all buyers' agents, Morrell uses his knowledge and experience to "drive prices down". He knows that most homes are sold below their true value[50].

It's a fact: Typical sellers' agents are no match for skilled buyers' agents, especially if sellers have been duped into selling by auction.

WARNING TO INEXPERIENCED INVESTORS: BE CAREFUL BUYING INVESTMENT PROPERTIES WITH THE HELP OF BUYERS' AGENTS ESPECIALLY WHERE THE SELLERS ARE PROPERTY DEVELOPERS[51]

REASON 81

Mortgagee sales and deceased estates use auctions

If auctions are so bad, why do mortgagees often sell by auction? The best way to answer that question is with another question: *Since when do banks care about the price of a distressed customer's home?*

As for those charged with looking after the affairs of the dead, their aim is the *appearance* of doing the right thing. "Transparency" attracts them. No one can accuse them of exploiting the estate. If that means properties get undersold, that's not their fault – or so they claim. How can anyone possibly criticise them for doing what most executors of estates do? It's only when – or if – beneficiaries insist on selling properties by a method that ensures the highest possible price that executors consider breaking from the traditional sale-by-auction method. And even then, their first concern is always how they appear to have acted. With the advertising of an auction campaign followed by a crowd of people at the auction, executors feel safe with the *appearance* they have created.

But as shrewd purchasers all know – one of the best places to nab bargains is at deceased estate or mortgagee-in-possession auctions.

In my mid-twenties, I bought several homes at deceased estate auctions. The executor was the NSW Public Trustee. Most homes were immediately "flipped" (re-sold) above the price I paid. I often re-sold them for 50% more than I paid at auction. Sometimes, I sold for twice what I paid. I'd buy at auction on Saturday and sell privately the next day[52].

I know from personal and profitable experience that auctions can mean very low prices.

REASON 82

Agents learn excuses to explain underselling

When Jim Grigoriou started his real estate career in Melbourne in 1982, he was expected to push auctions. Melbourne was dubbed "the auction capital of Australia". Jim says that's like saying Palermo is the Mafia capital of Italy.

From the outset, Jim was disturbed by auctions. He refused to tell sellers that "auction was the best way to sell". His beloved mother was the most ethical person in his life. She had brought him up to be scrupulously honest. At his auctions he kept being thanked by buyers who would have paid more than the auction system required them to pay.

When Jim expressed his concerns, his boss said, "Yes, I know, but that's an unfortunate side-effect of the auction system. There's nothing we can do about it."

Well, that wasn't correct. In 1992, upon Jim's urging, his boss attended a real estate course which outlined a system that showed how agents could get the highest price for their sellers without the deception of auctions. It meant more work, but neither Jim nor his boss cared. They were delighted. Now, they could sell homes for the best price.

Meanwhile most agents continued to deceive home-sellers into choosing auction.

Even when sellers discover that buyers would have paid more, instead of fixing the flawed system, the agents devise more slick lines.

The Real Estate Institute once ran a course called: "What Do You Say to the Vendor When the Purchaser is About to Sign the Contract and has a Bank Cheque For More Than the 10%? (Meaning he/she would have paid more)[53]."

REASON 83

Low price = big commission

For agents, getting paid is what real estate is all about. The best price rarely interests agents.

If agents really were concerned about getting the best price when they sell a home, they would not be obsessed with the sellers' lowest price. They would not ask the most common question agents ask about all home-sellers:

"HOW MUCH WILL THEY TAKE?"

Agents seldom ask: *How much can we get for the owners?*

Agents want to know your lowest price because that's when they get their commission. With auctions, they only need to get you the worst result you will accept. It's a classic case of: *Do as little as possible for as much as possible.*

Low effort, big reward. That's auctions.

Don't think a higher price means a higher commission for an agent. The difference to you between the buyers' highest price (BHP) and the price for which your home sells might be hundreds of thousands of dollars, but the difference to the agents is negligible.

If the agent gets an extra $100,000 for you, the agent gets an extra $2000. If the total commission is $34,000 (sale of $1.7 million) to the agent, $2000 is nothing. Your hundred thousand dollars (or more) will be quickly sacrificed so that the agent gets a commission today.

Whether you get a high price or a low price, the agent always gets a high commission.

It's easier to get a low price than a high price. That's why agents like auctions.

REASON 84

Art and literary auctions big losses for sellers

Agents love to cite how art and rare books are sold by auction, often for record prices.

I love literature. One of my favourite authors is Jack London. In 1903, he wrote *The Call of the Wild*, a book which became a classic and has been made into a movie at least three times, the latest in 2020 starring Harrison Ford.

Jack London also wrote *The Game*, a book about boxing. Many coaches insist their fighters read it. In 2004, the original manuscript of *The Game* was offered for auction in New York. It comprised 110 pages all in Jack London's own hand. For a lover of London, it was the find of a lifetime; but, of course, it would have been unaffordable for most Jack London fans. Floyd Mayweather or Mike Tyson would surely outbid anyone. It was expected to sell for upwards of $250,000 (US dollars).

I sent a friend to the auction. The highest I could afford was $127,000 (US dollars).

We bought it for $50,000[54].

Yes, $77,000 less than we would gladly have paid.

In 1999, Marilyn Monroe's dress – in which she sang "Happy Birthday" to President Kennedy – came up for auction. It sold for $1.15 million. The buyer, who estimated its value at $3 million, said, "We stole it[55]."

Back home, the bell that was used to signal the start and finish of the Rabbitoh's first rugby league match in 1908 came up for auction. The highest bidder was Russell Crowe. He paid $42,000. He was willing to pay $100,000[56].

When a Rubens masterpiece sold at auction in July 2002, it set a world record for a work of art at auction – $138 million[57].

The impression was created that items sell for high prices at auction.

But whether it's paintings, books or real estate, they often sell for higher prices at auction than owners expected. But, as with real estate, they rarely sell for the highest price.

One thing you can always count on: Almost everything sold by auction is undersold.

The buyers of the Rubens painting would gladly have paid double – another $138 million for a total of $276 million.

There is no sales method, other than auctions, where sellers get so savagely ripped off without realising it.

Sellers who are inexperienced and innocent get a torrid time at auctions. As has been shown in this book, they are innocent of the greatest truth – they lose as much as millions of dollars.

Ironically, the Rubens painting – whose owners *lost* $138 million by selling it at public auction – was called "The Massacre of the Innocents".

Art, books or property, it matters not: Auctions are the worst way to sell.

REASON 85

There are far better ways!

Auctions began about 2500 years ago in Greece. You'd think agents would have realised there are now many better ways to sell a home. Agents love to boast about how modern they are, and how they use technology; but they can't find a better system than the ancient art of auctions.

There are several better ways of selling a home than by public auction. For starters, you could hold a private auction – where interested buyers never see bids offered by other buyers. This is how many Scottish people sell their homes – and the Scots are renowned as great money managers. There are few public property auctions in Scotland. As their major newspaper, The Scotsman, wrote: "A property auction is one of the best ways to buy a house or flat at a discounted rate from the market value[58]."

Research shows that concealing the price of a home deters more than half the buyers[59]. And yet many agents tell sellers: "If you put a price on a home, it can only go down whereas an auction goes up." This proves their ignorance. Many times, homes are sold above asking prices. Buyers love to see an asking price. They are drawn to such homes.

The secret to getting the best price for a home is to not allow any buyers to know the amount offered by other buyers.

Selling by private tender or expressions-of-interest or sealed-bid auctions can ensure that sellers get the highest market price. As can hiring an agent who's a skilled negotiator.

If agents recommend a system of selling that's more than 2500 years old, tell them to get with the times. They arrived at your home in a car, not a chariot.

If an agent doesn't know a better way of selling than auction, sellers need to find a better agent.

REASON 86

At an auction there is no "true" salesperson!

Although most houses sell themselves (see Reason 4), with auctions, the houses must sell themselves. There is no "true" salesperson involved.

Most auction agents have never learned the art of selling. If they knew how to sell, they wouldn't sell by auction.

At auctions, the basic rules of selling are broken or flouted. These rules are vital to ensuring that sellers get the best result. Without these rules, sellers are at a huge disadvantage. Their homes are almost guaranteed to be undersold.

If you want to sell your home for the highest possible price, you cannot afford to hire agents who break the rules of selling or agents who don't know how to sell. If you want to sell your home – rather than just wait for a buyer to buy it – the first thing you need is a true salesperson.

Here are six important selling rules. All missing to some degree at auctions.

1. PROSPECTING

Good salespeople search for leads. They make plenty of "cold calls". Auction agents, however, rarely do any prospecting, especially "cold calls" (they are too scared to approach strangers).

Most auction salespeople are lazy. Rather than follow up leads, they convince sellers to pay for expensive advertising campaigns.

When you hire an auction salesperson you are hiring someone who'd prefer to spend your money than their energy.

Don't let yourself be financially punished by lazy salespeople.

2. QUALIFYING

True selling is qualifying customers. Auction agents bypass this vital step completely. They rarely discover the highest price buyers are prepared to pay. Many times, auction agents never meet the buyers before they buy. They discover the buyers' highest price *after* the buyer has bought the home. Another reason homes are undersold.

3. PRESENTING

Most auction agents know little or nothing about the homes they are selling. Their "presentation" ranges from mediocre to hopeless. They stand at the front door of a home handing out brochures and floor plans.

At best, auction agents are tour guides, not salespeople.

4. OBJECTIONS

When buyers are considering purchasing a product, they often have concerns. In selling, these concerns are called "objections". One of the great skills of true salespeople is "overcoming objections". Auction agents barely speak with buyers, so they rarely hear their objections, let alone overcome them. Buyers talk themselves out of homes that are being auctioned because skilled salespeople are absent.

5. HOLDING

When buyers like a home, skilled agents "hang on" to those buyers. But not with auctions. You can see it at any "open inspection". Keen buyers may approach the agent who is either too busy with "tyre-kickers" or too worried about getting to the next open inspection. The agents tell the buyers to "make sure you are at the auction". And so, these "hot buyers" wander off to see other homes. They go cold on the home they like. They buy another home because the agent was too incompetent to "hold them" while they were hot. The saying "Strike while the iron is hot" is one of the fundamental principles of great salespeople. It barely exists with auction agents.

6. CLOSING

The final stage of the sales process is "closing the deal". This is where a salesperson, having given a skilled presentation, persuades customers to buy the product offered. Yes, the sale is *closed.*

Yelling at someone in front of a crowd is not the best way to close a sale. And it is certainly not the best way to get the best result for home-sellers.

Don't hire agents who don't follow the vital rules of selling.

Don't auction.

REASON 87

Auctions are illegal

Public real estate auctions – as conducted by most agents – are almost certainly illegal.

Agents have a fiduciary duty – a legal obligation – to "act in the best interests of sellers".

According to several lawyers[60], if agents tell sellers: "Auction is the best way to sell a home for the best price," and those homes are *not* sold for the best price – as happens at most auctions – the agent has clearly not acted in the best interests of the sellers.

The agent has knowingly given negligent and deceptive advice to the sellers – which directly caused their home to be undersold.

Anyone who has sold a home by auction could be entitled to a REFUND OF COMMISSION paid to the agent.

This reason may cause agents to stop doing auctions.

Or, at least to start telling the truth, namely that:

MOST HOMES SOLD AT AUCTION ARE UNDERSOLD.

REASON 88

Sellers lose $100,000 average

In 2022, the average price of a home in Australia was close to $1,000,000. The average amount homes are undersold at auction is close to 10% of their true value.

Therefore, a million-dollar home will likely sell at auction for about $900,000.

As we have seen, being happy about a sale doesn't make it a good sale. It doesn't mean you sold for the best price.

The best price is the *highest value* of your home. That should always be your aim: nothing but the best. Anything less than true value is a loss.

When you think of the word "auction" – especially if an agent is urging you to sell by auction – always think: UNDERSOLD.

Given that the average price of a home in the nation is close to $1,000,000 and given that homes sold at auction commonly sell for 10% below their true value, here's what to remember …

The average homeowner who sells by auction
UNDERSELLS THEIR HOME BY $100,000.

And that is Reason Number 88 for never selling by auction. You are near certain to lose at least $100,000. In big cities, with average prices double that figure in many suburbs, your loss by selling at auction is likely to be two or three times $100,000. That's $200,000 or $300,000.

Like all the 88 reasons, this reason should be enough to ensure you never sell by public auction.

If you need support to find a good agent or more information on how to sell your home for the best price, please contact Jenman Support on 1800 1800 18 or support@jenman.com.au.

A message to agents who may hurl abuse over this book.

THE GREAT DEBATE CHALLENGE

Here's an offer to agents who support auctions. Forget the abuse, I will ignore it.

Instead of abuse, put forth one of your own to debate me civilly and courteously.

I will debate any high-profile figure – ideally, a chief auctioneer of a major franchise group. Or any chest-thumper to whom the media give time to spruik the so-called merits of auctions.

The title of the debate will be:

"IS PUBLIC AUCTION THE BEST WAY TO SELL A HOME?"

The debate will be judged by homeowners with no link to agents.

The debate will be held in a meeting hall with at least 500 homeowners in attendance. Plus, live-streamed on-line.

The costs of promoting and staging the debate will be paid in advance by both debaters. But the loser of the debate will pay all costs, thus reimbursing 50% of the costs to the winner.

The loser of the debate will donate **$100,000 (ONE HUNDRED THOUSAND DOLLARS)** to a charity of the winner's choice.

The loser of the debate will provide a link to the debate on the home page of their website so that consumers can view the debate.

Any takers?

Please email neil@jenman.com.au.

PART 2

2 REASONS YOU MIGHT AUCTION

REASON 1

When the decision is not all yours - estates etc

If you oversee an estate, and beneficiaries or other parties insist on using auction as a method and you cannot convince them that auction is the worst way to sell, then sell by auction.

Make sure you give a copy of this book to all parties associated with the estate. And make it clear that **auction means underselling the property.** If they are too lazy or too arrogant or too busy (or whatever reason) to make time to find out why auctions do not get the best price, I can understand you saying: "You are making the wrong decision but go ahead. I can't be bothered arguing with you."

REASON 2

Help the nice agent

If you feel sorry for a nice agent, maybe you will be prepared to sell your home for a low price and pay the agent a big commission.

Plus, you can pay for all that advertising which enables these agents to promote themselves at your expense.

Your advertising money also enables agents to find more leads and earn themselves more commission from other sales – all thanks to your kindness and generosity.

Make sure the agent appreciates you. Gratitude is essential.

PART 3

7 REASONS TO BUY AT AUCTION

REASON 1

You can buy under-value

You can buy properties at public auction well below the price you are prepared to pay.

Not every property, of course. Sometimes you will go to an auction and the bidding will surpass your maximum price. In those cases, you miss out.

Be careful not to waste too much money on reports; use your common sense. When you understand property, it's not hard to do many checks yourself thereby saving hundreds of dollars in reports. But even if you do lose as much as a couple of thousand dollars on homes you don't buy, when you do have a win, it will usually be worth it.

Sometimes, buyers pay millions below what they are willing to pay. And some buyers buy at auction and immediately "flip" the property and make hundreds of thousands of dollars profit.

Buy low and sell high – that's the success formula for investing.

Auctions give you the chance to buy low – often very low.

REASON 2

Less competition

When you are buying at auction – especially in areas where auctions are uncommon – you have less competition from other buyers.

In addition, many buyers are not able to buy under the harsh contractual conditions usually applicable with auctions. Few sellers realise that making the contract tough deters buyers. Indeed, the best buyers – those willing to pay the most – often *need* conditions.

Without those buyers competing with you, the price is often much lower.

REASON 3

You *can* create "conditions"

The auction system thrives on intimidation. Most buyers never challenge the terms under which homes are offered at auction. They just walk away. But if you request some mild conditions added to the contract you will often get a favourable response. This is especially true if you hint that you will pay a higher price than other bidders.

You should also make sellers aware – politely and humbly, not as a threat – that the addition of requested conditions will decide your ability to bid. If refused, you will not be able to bid.

In most cases sellers will allow mild conditions to be included in the contract – such as, for example, paying 5% deposit. Or a longer settlement time – say 10 weeks instead of six weeks.

Remember the saying: *If you don't ask, the answer is always no.*

Most buyers are too intimidated to ask. They just avoid auctions, which means they miss a chance to buy cheaply.

REASON 4

You can chase buyers away

It's easy to discourage buyers from bidding at auctions. You can ask questions and raise concerns in front of the crowd or use more unsavoury tactics favoured by experienced buyers or their agents. It's not pleasant to ruin the sellers' chances of a good price – especially for spurious reasons – so these tactics are not revealed here. I don't want to teach unethical conduct.

Still, if you have a genuine worry about a property and you raise it publicly at the auction, it often causes other buyers to drop out, leaving you to buy cheaply.

REASON 5

The best agents to buy from!

Agents who push auctions are usually short-term thinkers focused on a quick commission. They rarely get the best price for the owners, but they sure get the cheapest price for the buyers.

It doesn't matter what method of sale is being used, agents who push auctions will undersell homes by any method. Offer a low price today and their eyes will light up at the thought of a commission today.

When you see an agent who pushes auctions, you are seeing an agent who undersells homes.

REASON 6

You can plan ahead

A fixed date is more beneficial for buyers than sellers. There are so many disadvantages for sellers in making buyers wait weeks to buy a home, it's a wonder any sellers agree to auction.

Still, from a buyer's perspective, having the auction tied to a set date not only deters many other buyers, but it also allows you to plan.

Everything is mapped out for you – all ready to buy the property at a set time with conditions laid out. Although misled or misinformed, auction sellers are serious sellers. They rarely change their minds before auction and are locked in from the time of sale. It gives buyers a level of certainty they don't get in other forms of sale.

REASON 7

You can earn a fortune

As mentioned, I have bought dozens of properties at auction, sometimes for half their true value. Many of these properties were deceased estates auctioned by the Public Trustee.

Often, I renovated homes before re-selling them. But soon I found so many homes at auction for low prices, I could instantly re-sell them at their true value.

These opportunities are still available today.

Anyone prepared to research prices in various areas can earn a small fortune buying properties under-value at auction and then selling them for their true value.

Please don't think: "If it was that easy, everyone would do it." That's what people often said to me. They would ask: "If you are buying properties under-value and re-selling them as little as hours later for their true value, why isn't everyone doing it?"

I always gave the same answer: "I don't know why no one else is doing it."

But I do know that the main reason I became an agent was because I wanted to show homeowners how to get the best price for their homes. In my years as an agent, no one bought a home from my office under its value. I told all sellers: "If you want the best price, don't auction." I told buyers: "If you want a bargain, go to the auctions and then sell with me." Many took that advice and did well.

If you are interested in property, you can still earn a fortune buying homes at auction. If you feel uncomfortable taking advantage of misinformed people, stick with deceased estates. Or better still, become a good agent and make your fortune protecting home-sellers by helping them get the highest price.

It's great to make a profit for yourself and your clients.

ACKNOWLEDGEMENTS

No one does – or has done – more for me in my life than my wife, Reiden. As I say to her almost daily: *Thank you for marrying me.* Without your support, I could not do half of what I do. You are my inspiration, my helper, my minder and, of course, my best friend. For almost 30 years, you have given me what I have always longed for – security. Although it's rarely mentioned, thank you for saving my life back in 2006. The doctor said "nothing to worry about" but you demanded another opinion. You were right; it was something to worry about. Clark Level 4 melanoma is serious. Without you, I would not be here today. For those of you with changing skin moles or lesions, get them checked, please. Your loved ones need you.

My sincere thanks to the wonderful people who work at Jenman Support for giving consumers real estate support they can trust. Some of you – such as Sandra Adler and Heather Goodman – are approaching 20 years of wonderful service. I appreciate you very much. My long-standing and dedicated secretary of many years, Debbie Matthews, thank you so much for looking after me. I feel so good with you in my life. My beautiful daughter Haley who is often the first voice sellers or buyers hear when they call 1800 1800 18, no wonder we get high praise with you as their first contact; thank you for your love and devotion. When you were a toddler, people said, "All Haley wants is a hug." You haven't changed and I am so proud of you. My son Alec, who went from school to assisting me to help real estate consumers, you are a "natural" at supporting home-sellers and buyers. As with your sister, the praise we get about your care and concern for consumers fills me with pride. Please keep figuring out how we can help more people. Thousands of people sell their homes each week, all of whom would be better off if they contacted us before they contacted an agent. Help us to figure out how to reach them all, please.

Thank you to those few agents who support me. Especially Jim Grigoriou who has been a loyal supporter and friend for 30 years. And, of course, my great friend Michael Kies, Australia's best real estate trainer to whom we often give the toughest job of all – finding good agents for home-sellers. Your loyalty, dedication and integrity are an example to the real estate world.

Nothing would be possible without the support of the people who matter most in this real estate world – the home-sellers and buyers. From close to two million copies of my various books, sellers and buyers have been my staunch supporters. Agents might disagree with me, but I cannot recall a word of criticism from an honest consumer. Perhaps that's because I have always done what my first boss, an old-fashioned estate agent called Reg Baglow, taught me to do back in 1972 – work hard and always do what's best for the clients. *It worked, Reg!*

When agents say I am "betraying" the industry with my revelations, I reply: Agents are not my customers. The agents' customers are my customers. Sellers and buyers are the ones to whom I give my loyalty. The greatest "payment" I receive is trust and appreciation from consumers. Nothing could make me betray those who matter most in the real estate world – the sellers and the buyers. My sincere thanks to all of you who contact me. And please, never think that you are a "bother". The more questions you ask before you sell your home, the more research you do – and the more you insist on finding the best agent for your home – the more likely you are to get the best price. Your home is probably your greatest financial asset and I admire you for having the intelligence and the commitment to protect its value.

My thanks to all those who have helped bring this book to fruition including Annabel Adair for her usual brilliant editing and proof-reading, Allen Larkin of GR8 Graphics for his meticulous work with the layout and, again, my wife, Reiden Jenman, and my secretary,

Debbie Matthews, for reading the manuscript multiple times through its many edits and re-writes. I know I have greatly tested your patience, but you have passed brilliantly.

Thank you to the home-sellers who read this book. I hope it will save you the equivalent of a year or more of your annual salary. I welcome your comments and stories. Best of all, before you sell, I hope you contact Jenman Support because we will be proud to help you. As my son Alec is proud of saying: We will never ask you for money, we will never ask you to sign anything, and we will always fight to protect your interests. Surely that's worth contacting us.

Whatever you choose to do, I wish you the very best outcome possible.

Neil Jenman. February 2022.

SOURCE NOTES

INTRODUCTION

1. Based on a selling fee of 2% on a sale of $11 million. Some agents charge as much as 3.3% which would bring the commission up to $363,000.

2. Most Real Estate Institutes have a code of ethics, the first of which is that it is unethical to criticise other agents. Even if an agent is robbing a home at an open inspection, it would be unethical to call the police. Protecting each other is the sacred rule among agents.

REASON 4

3. Many years ago, in Perth, I attended an open-for-inspection with the then managing director of the Roy Weston Group. At first, we couldn't find the sales representative. Then we heard what sounded like a soft humming noise coming from the living room. We discovered the rep fast asleep on the lounge. We gently placed our business cards on his chest – and tip-toed out.

4. Based on the author's extensive research. Recently, two different auction agents have told me that the final sale price at their auctions is always less than the highest bidder's highest price. When I clarified with them that this meant "100 per cent of your auction sales are undersold", they agreed. They also said it didn't matter because "The vendors are happy". But, of course, they are only happy because they are unaware.

REASON 6

5. Roy Morgan online survey conducted from 13–22 April 2021, with 1267 Australian men and women aged 14 and over. Respondents were asked: "As I say different occupations, could you please say – from what you know or have heard – which rating best describes how you, yourself, would rate or score people in various occupations for honesty and ethical standards (Very High, High, Average, Low, Very Low)?"

REASON 7

6. The book Relax and Sell More Real Estate by Graham White who was reportedly a senior real estate sales trainer for the LJ Hooker network. Chapter 8, "At the Auction", page 214. White writes: "The vendors and purchasers. Remember, they are even more nervous than you are. It is your job to wander around and keep them nervous." Published by Team Training Sydney, 1986. ISBN 947075 00 3.

REASON 9

7. Tim Fletcher of Fletcher and Parker Real Estate.

8. In December 2017 in the Federal Court in Melbourne, Fletcher and Parker Real Estate (Balwyn) Pty Ltd was fined a total of $880,000 being $40,000 for each of 22 properties that were inspected by Consumer Affairs officers and found to be massively falsely underquoted. Justice Bernard Murphy said underquoting was "a widespread problem" in Melbourne estate agencies.

   Justice Murphy also said that Fletcher and Parker "had a cavalier attitude to its responsibilities".

   The evidence included:

   The quote of the week in one of the Fletcher and Parker sales meeting was: "market the f— out of it and then underquote the shit out of it – good vendor management".

   Sales staff were at least once provided training which focused on cases where underquoting had seemingly led to a high sales price and a significant spike in interest.

   Sales agents describing Consumer Affairs as "a toothless tiger" – as they would after years of brazenly deceiving the public and abusing anyone who dared to criticise them (including this author).

9. County Court of Victoria, Monday 5 February 2001, Judge Ian Robertson. See also "Estate agents sued over price estimate", Angela O'Connor, The Age, 26 August 2000; "Judge rejects auction claim", Angela O'Connor, The Sunday Age, 11 February 2001; "Barrister loses auction lawsuit", Kelly Ryan, County Court Reporter, Herald Sun, Tuesday 6 February 2001.

REASON 10

10. University Hospitals – The Science of Health. The Top 5 Most Stressful Life Events and How to Handle Them. 3 July 2015. These events are: death of a loved one; divorce; moving house; major illness or injury; job loss.

11. See Source Note 6.

REASON 11

12. Perhaps the most widely accepted and most well-known point in property valuation is what's called "the willing seller, willing buyer theory". This theory is accepted around the world. It was believed to have originated in Roman times. A good definition is from Wikipedia which reads: "The fair market value is the price at which the property would change hands between a willing buyer and a willing seller, neither being under any compulsion to buy or to sell and both having reasonable knowledge of relevant facts."

Obviously, at a public auction, sellers are denied a "relevant fact" – namely, the amount the buyers are willing to pay. Hence the reason properties are undersold at auctions.

REASON 23

13. Legend has it that there was once a famous Russian mule trainer called Ivan. He travelled from village to village claiming he could train the most stubborn mules. When he arrived in a village, a local farmer would bring forth the most difficult mule in the district. The mule would be taken to the town square where a crowd of locals would gather to watch the famous mule trainer. Ivan would walk around the mule several times – he and the mule eye-balling each other. After a few minutes, Ivan would walk to the side of the square and return with a large wooden mallet. He would give the mule an almighty whack between the eyes. The crowd would gasp in horror as the mule staggered backwards, its eyes rolling. Invariably, the mule's owner would scream, "You could have killed him!" Ivan would turn to the crowd and say, "To train mules, first you must get their attention." And so it is with agents and home-buyers today in Australia. The reason for underquoting to buyers is simple: First you must get their attention.
14. Interview with the author in Melbourne, 18 January 2020. Also present at the interview – which was recorded with permission – was the author's son Alec Jenman and two other friends of the author. Interview lasted one hour and 40 minutes. The agent made many frank admissions including that all salespeople in the company were instructed to give "dummy offers" to all sellers after their first open inspection.
15. Tom Panos.

REASON 24

16. Enzo Raimondo.
17. Derek Guille.
18. Castran Gilbert, South Yarra. The author has a copy of an invoice dated 20 October 2000 sent to the owners of a property auctioned in Cromwell Street, South Yarra, which includes such charges as "Auction attendance Ted – $25"; "Auction attendance Peter – $25"; "Auction attendance Ron – $30".

REASON 27

19. Australian home-buyers would save tens of millions of dollars if state governments enacted one simple piece of legislation – making it mandatory for sellers to provide building reports and compliance certificates etc and warranting that these reports were accurate. Such mandatory "disclosure" laws are now common throughout the world, especially in the United States. The only place in Australia where such laws exist is the ACT.

REASON 32

20. Article in the Courier-Mail on 18 June 2021: "Market madness: 'If you don't sell at auction ... you're a lunatic'" by Elizabeth Tilley. Quote attributed to Jason Adcock, real estate agent, was: "It's the most transparent way of determining the value of a property in this heated market. If you don't go to auction in the current market, you're a lunatic." Of course, as anyone who fully understands auctions is aware, the transparency claim is only partial. At auctions sellers are severely disadvantaged in having to reveal the lowest price they will accept whereas buyers can conceal the highest price they will pay. Therefore, homes are so massively undersold at auctions, especially high-end homes, Mr Adcock's claimed specialty. This is a point that Mr Adcock either doesn't understand or doesn't reveal.

REASON 33

21. See Source Note 32.

REASON 34

22. Openn (sic) Negotiation. Founded 2016 in Claremont WA. www.openn.com.au
23. Prospectus of Initial Public Offering by Openn Negotiation Limited (ACN 612 329 754). On page 3, Chairperson's Letter by Non-executive Chairperson Wayne Zekulich, there are three erroneous claims in the first four paragraphs:

Claim 1: "providing the best possible property sales outcome for the seller, the buyer and the agent".

Claim 2: "achieve market value for a property".

Claim 3: "ensures price maximisation for the seller".

Perhaps the most absurd and most misleading of many claims throughout the prospectus is this one (at the bottom of page 12): "... auctions involve full price transparency to both vendors and buyers and result in a property selling for 'market price' (i.e., the price that buyers are willing to pay on that day)". As already covered in this book, auctions do not involve full price transparency. (See Reason 33 – THE TRANSPARENCY TRAP.) Also, "the price that buyers are willing to pay" is clearly intended to imply that this is the best price the buyers are willing to pay when that is not the case. As already pointed out, in most auctions (all auctions according to some agents), the price paid by the buyers is well below their best price which means, of course, that homes are undersold at auctions.

REASON 35

24. The three costs on a $2 million property sale would typically be: The commission of about 2.5% = $50,000; the marketing costs of about 1% = $20,000; and the undersold amount (which according to the author's research averages 8%) = $160,000.

    The total of these three costs is $230,000 (likely to be conservative).

REASON 36

25. Based on a sale price of $1.5 million at a commission rate of 2%.

REASON 37

26. Webinar for agents held by Openn Negotiation, Tuesday 3 August 2021. Entitled "How to Sell More in Less Time with Openn Negotiation". Hosted by Will Ainsworth, Head of Growth and Training Aus/NZ. From recording (and transcript) of event given to author.

REASON 38

27. Relax and Sell More Real Estate by Graham White 1986. Published by Team Training Sydney. ISBN 0 947075 00 3. Chapter 17, "Open For Inspections", page 135: "If it is a property that pulls well, and we are meeting a lot of new people, then the worst thing we can do is sell it". Although this book was published in 1986, such an attitude is even more common today.

28. James Packham of Harcourts Packham in Marion, SA. Training video for agents. Circa 2019. In a 45-second clip, Packham, who speaks like a used car salesman, describes himself as "one of the most recognised real estate personalities in South Australia" and says the following: "If you're in real estate, open for inspections are one of the best sources to meet people selling real estate. A lot of people that rock up at an open for inspection come with a trade-in. Not only are they looking to buy property, they need to sell property as part of the transaction. And a mistake that agents make is that the minute there is any level of excitement around a listing they sell it at the first open. But what you need to do is focus on maximising the number of opens over the course of a campaign. So why not consider booking a 'best offer by' or an auction campaign even slipping in the occasional midweek viewing and then you can 5X the number of buyer sellers that you're meeting and that's really going to open up your pipeline and how you're going to meet sellers in your community."

    Again, it's clear: The main purpose of open inspections is not to find buyers, it's to find more sellers. The hapless sellers whose homes are open-for-inspection have no idea they are being used as a source of listing leads for agents. They think an open-for-inspection is designed to find buyers. But as most open inspections last a mere 30 minutes (out of 10,080 minutes per week) it does not give buyers much time.

Buyers have complained to this author that they are prevented from buying homes until agents have done what James Packham suggests – "maximising the number of opens". If buyers complain to the owners (as they should), dodgy agents will reply: "We need to hold lots of 'opens' so that we can make sure we don't miss any buyers." But, of course, the buyers who want to buy at the first open house are usually long gone by the time of the fourth or fifth open house. Agents then say to the owners: "The market is telling us you need to drop your price."

29. The Real Estate Office Manual by Alan Fleming. Published by the Real Estate Institute of Australia Ltd, Canberra, with which are affiliated the Real Estate Institutes of New South Wales, Victoria, Queensland, South Australia, Western Australia, Tasmania, Northern Territory and the ACT. ISBN: 0909784620.

REASON 39

30. See Source Note 27.

REASON 40

31. The auctions for the sale of the houses on 2020 season of The Block took place on Saturday 21 November 2020. The final episode aired on Sunday 22 November 2020. An estimated 1.8 million viewers watched the home (located at 360 New Street, Brighton, Victoria), which had been renovated by contestants Jimmy and Tam, sell for an astonishing $4,256,000, which was $966,000 above the reserve price of $3,290,000.

    The amount above the reserve (plus a $100,000 bonus for being the winners) gave Jimmy and Tam the most prize money ever won on the popular show – $1,066,000.

    The highest bidder was a petite 28-year-old woman, Emese Fajk. She was described as a cyber security expert. Many people wondered how such a young woman could afford $4,256,000. As happens at most auctions, the agents had not "qualified" any of the bidders. This woman was later exposed as a known con-woman. She did not pay a deposit, nor did she settle the purchase. So, what happened? Nothing. How do you get someone who has no money and yet bids an amount of $4,256,000 at an auction to pay the amount they bid? It's not possible.

    Of the nearly two million viewers, almost none realised that the winning bidder was unable to afford the home. And even later, when it was revealed she had failed to buy the home, few people would have realised that she did what anyone can do at the end of an auction before the contracts have been signed – walk away.

To their immense credit, the producers of The Block honoured Jimmy and Tam's prize money.

REASON 43

32. In 2006, Louis Christopher was the public spokesperson for Australian Property Monitors, owned by Fairfax. He regularly appeared on television. When he exposed the fake auction clearance rates, the backlash from agents, especially the Real Estate Institute of Victoria (REIV), was savage. Louis broke the long-standing real estate industry rule: If the industry pays you, they own you. Those who dare to expose wrongdoings (which are massive and widespread) risk becoming certain outcasts. They lose their jobs; if they own a business, it is severely impacted such as being black-banned or boycotted. Plus, they face horrendous abuse, the besmirching of their name with lies and rumours and even physical threats (as this author has received). Sadly, the public rarely acknowledge the courage of those who speak out to protect consumers. All these ramifications are the reason why almost no one dares publicly criticise real estate agents (especially near-sacred auctioneers) or those who profit from the industry, such as advertisers or research companies.

In 2006, fed up with what he was witnessing, Louis Christopher refused to remain silent. He was no longer prepared to cover up the truth. And so, he publicly revealed that auction clearance rates were deliberately inflated to create a false appearance that auctions were far more successful than in reality.

As punishment, he was immediately suspended by Fairfax Senior Management. At no stage was it ever said by his employer or anyone within the real estate industry that what Louis revealed was incorrect. No, just that he was not allowed to be truthful about auctions. His job description may as well have been, "You will willingly participate in the deception of the public regarding the merits of auctions. You must never criticise or denigrate auctions."

In addition to having his employment suspended, Fairfax told Louis Christopher they would "censor his newsletters" from then onwards. In other words, they would replace his truths with the real estate industry's lies.

Louis Christopher was told that he had "no career prospects with Fairfax" as he had "burnt the bridges with the senior executives" (September 2006).

Said Louis in 2021:

"I refused to accept the newsletter condition and immediately resigned. The b------s then turned around and demanded to cut my payout in half or they would immediately dismiss me without any employee payout at all. Regretfully, I accepted that on recommendation of my lawyer. My lawyer warned me that they would likely dirty my name out there making future employment choices difficult if I fought them."

Although out of a job and with "no career prospects", Louis started his own research company, SQM Research. As mentioned, Louis Christopher and SQM Research are today the most trusted and respected property researchers (by those "in the know") in Australia. SQM Research employs 18 full-time staff. Many major companies and institutions, including the Reserve Bank, are clients of SQM Research. They are Australia's trusted property researchers.

Today, the auction clearance rates released by most of the well-known real estate research companies are still chronically and deliberately misleading. In 2021, Louis Christopher said: "They do not deserve any quarter! Misleading people the way they do is bordering on evil."

"I still fight the fight on auction clearance rates. Domain, REA and CL refuse to amend their flawed methodology." They release flawed information because it pleases their masters who pay them – the real estate agents.

Louis Christopher knows, from personal experience, that misleading and often fraudulent property information causes immense harm to consumers. Buyers and sellers trust the statistics and unknowingly make major financial errors based on concocted information and, worse, the cover-up and concealment of vital truths. In the 1980s, Louis witnessed the impact of false real estate claims when his elderly grandparents were ripped off in real estate. Louis Christopher is the only major researcher (known to this author) with the courage to say that regurgitating the industry's lies is tantamount to "evil".

Email from Louis Christopher to author 23 July 2021, in response to questions regarding the backlash he received after exposing the deliberate falsification of auction statistics.

REASON 44

33. This figure is likely conservative. The author's own research, conducted consistently since 1984, shows that almost all (100%) family home-buyers detest auctions. Of course, those who realise how much they can save by buying below the price they are willing to pay will tolerate auctions for that reason only. Still, they detest the process, including the near constant deception, the half-truths, the lack of communication and the rudeness in the lead-up to auction. And then, as with sellers, buyers detest the pressure that's applied to them at the auction.

    The only buyers who openly said they like auctions are investors or bargain-hunters.

A study conducted by the Swinburne University of Technology in Melbourne revealed that only 4% of home-buyers nominated auction as their preferred method of buying a home. (Centre for Urban and Social Research, Swinburne University of Technology, "The Melbourne Home Buyers Survey", 1992.)

One of the basic tenets of good sales procedure is to please customers. It is often referred to as "make it easy for buyers to buy" as well as making the process pleasant. There is no more difficult or unpleasant way to buy real estate than public auction.

Therefore, to openly promote a system of sale that most buyers despise is not just contrary to basic sales procedure, it defies common sense. But then, as repeatedly stated in this book, auctions are not done for the reasons that agents claim (to get the best price). Auctions are done because they suit agents. To repeat the words from a Real Estate Institute training manual: "Auctions are the fastest and best conditioning method."

REASON 47

34. The author's researchers contacted agents in the three eastern cities of Melbourne, Sydney and Brisbane. The researchers said, "If we are considering selling a home in your area, would you mind answering some questions about your service?" Most agents agreed to answer questions, although some indignantly said, "What is this, a job interview?" – but that's exactly what it should be. As a homeowner you hire someone for the "job" of selling your home. You should interview agents as you would interview a job applicant.

All agents in the survey were asked if they had much experience at negotiating. All claimed to be experienced and competent negotiators. When asked what courses they had taken on the topic of negotiation, they cited auction training courses or real estate sales seminars. None had attended a training course (of which there are many) about negotiation in business. Most surprising (and alarming) was the answer to the question: "What books have you read about negotiation?" From one hundred agents, none had read a book on negotiation.

NOTE: If you would like some suggested "interview questions" that home-sellers should ask real estate agents, please contact support@jenman.com.au or call 1800 1800 18.

REASON 49

35. Home owned by Brian White, Chairman of Ray White real estate group. Home at 32 Sutherland Avenue, Ascot (in Brisbane). Scheduled for auction 17 July 2021. Sold approximately 10 days before auction date. According to the Courier-Mail, Saturday 10 July, "a bidding war erupted between four buyers". In the

article entitled "Brisbane's own White House sells for $10m after bidding war" (by Elizabeth Tilley), it stated that the owner was "determined not to let the property go under the hammer" and "a multiple offer situation ensued". Of course, when each of the four buyers are unaware of the amount being bid by the other three buyers, it forces all buyers to offer their highest price rather than offering slightly more than the most recent bid.

Clearly, Mr White and his agents from Ray White New Farm (Matt Lancashire) and Ray White Ascot (Dwight Ferguson) used the best strategy to ensure their boss got the best price. If only all Ray White agents did the same for all their sellers, then sellers would certainly sell for the highest price, just like Mr White did – instead of being undersold at public auction as happens at Ray White auctions.

REASON 53

36. Auctions held in Melbourne and Sydney on Saturday 5 June 2021.
37. On Saturday 30 March 2020, there were 21 auctions in Perth. None sold at auction. The auction clearance rate released by the industry for that day was 30%.

REASON 55

38. The incidents of traffic, weather, accidents, sleeping-in, even the proverbial flat tyre and other rare events in modern times are just a few of many ridiculous reasons that can cause buyers to run late and often arrive after the auction is over. Of course, if the property has been sold – as is often the case – it doesn't matter to the agent. A sale is a sale. And, as explained many times, agents get a big commission no matter the amount of the price. Of course, when buyers turn up late to an auction and claim they would have paid more than the selling price, the agents do not inform the sellers. They don't even try to negotiate with the bidders who bought the property to see if they would consider a financial incentive to back out. For example, if a property sells for $1.5 million and another buyer who arrived late was willing to pay $1.8 million, the "late buyer" could offer the actual buyer as much as $300,000 to back out. These stories rarely get shared with the public. The phenomenon of "late buyers" is far more common than most people realise. Indeed, it's one of the disadvantages (to sellers) of public auctions that seldom occurs to sellers. I had been working in the industry for 20 years before I realised how often higher paying buyers arrive late at an auction. Oh sure, I always knew that holding an auction on a set day at a set time caused some buyers to avoid the auction altogether, but it was not until I bought at an auction and was offered thousands of dollars more to "back out" just minutes after the auction that I began to realise how often such incidents occur.

Many auction agents will deny that such incidents happen. Or they will claim – as is common with many of the reasons not to sell by auction – that "this has never happened to us". And yet while agents may deny that any higher paying buyers have ever turned up after the auction when the property had been massively undersold, no agent could deny that, under "normal auction conditions", such incidents are entirely possible. One of the "advantages" touted by on-line real estate auction companies – such as Openn Negotiation – is that the agent can adjust the finishing time of the auction to suit the circumstances of the buyers. So, even if the buyers did have an incident that caused them a delay, the agent can pause the auction. Of course, this still does not mean (as Openn Negotiation widely and erroneously claims) that on-line auctions get the best price. A public auction – where all buyers can see the offers made by all other buyers – is hugely disadvantageous to home-sellers.

REASON 60

39. "Nancy" is a pseudonym for Ning Widjaja. Story as told by her to the author. At the time of writing, Ning was a real estate representative with Forsyth Real Estate in Willoughby. The principal of Forsyth Real Estate is James Snodgrass, a person who is honest and frank in discussions with this author. Mr Snodgrass openly admits that homes are undersold at auction – "all the time".

40. "Stephen" is a pseudonym for Simon Nolan. As discussed with the author in a recorded (with disclosure) phone call, 30 July 2019. At the time of publication, Simon is a real estate representative with McGrath Real Estate in Maroubra. His website says that he and his team pride themselves on "putting their client's (sic) interests first". Despite industry peer pressure, Simon is above most agents for ethics and honesty.

REASON 62

41. Relax and Sell More Real Estate by Graham White 1986. Published by Team Training Sydney. ISBN 0 947075 00 3. Chapter 28, "Auction Section Part 6 – Between Signing and Selling", page 216.

REASON 63

42. David Morrell of Morrell and Koren Buyers' Advocates. Their stated aim is to make sure buyers do not pay one dollar more than sellers are willing to accept. Considering that most sellers' agents are hopeless negotiators, the claims of Morrell and Koren carry a great deal of veracity. They boast, "We are very very good at saving you money."

    In 2004, Morrell wrote a book. He explained why agents often treat buyers with near contempt – unless, unless, unless – wait for it: UNLESS THE BUYERS

HAVE A HOUSE FOR SALE. And here's the catch for buyers: If you have sold your home and you have a few million dollars in cash, don't think that will get you first class treatment. On the contrary, the fact that you have sold your home means the agents can only get one sale from you (when you buy). But a buyer who has not yet sold means two sales for the agent. Plus, as Morrell repeatedly points out in his book, nothing excites a typical agent more than the thought of a new listing. Therefore, if buyers want to be treated well, they simply cannot afford to be truthful. Writes Morrell, "My advice is to always suggest to the agent that you have a house for sale. The agent isn't necessarily always telling you the truth, so only tell them what you can use to your advantage. The name of the game must always be to win and buy the property for the cheapest price."

David Morrell's book is called Real Estate Myths Exploded. ISBN 0 7344 0719 X.

Disclosure: This author has no connection whatsoever to Morrell and Koren and, to the best of his recollection, has never spoken with Morrell or anyone from their buyers' agency.

43. Article in The Sun-Herald, 3 June 2001 – "This man earns $40,000 in just 20 minutes … being a pain" by Cindy Martin.

44. From the Morrell and Koren website, "If it's an auction, we'll control it."

REASON 72

45. "Why Women Are Better Negotiators Than Men", HER Magazine, 18 April 2018, by Kelly Stickel.

"Women tend to be better negotiators than men because they are more thoughtful; they are active listeners and are able to show more of an open-mind. They can also utilize their empathetic side, come off as more relatable, and using those skill sets they get the job done. If you're a woman who wants to become better at negotiating, don't reject your natural tendencies; embrace them."

Kelly Stickel is the founder and CEO of Remodista, a social think tank examining global retail and fintech disruption.

46. Author's own experience. When speaking with agents, it is consistently the female agents who seem to achieve better prices than the males. While it is relatively easy to get male agents to "reveal all", it's females who often say, "I am sorry, but I must not reveal that information." Of course, some males are good negotiators, but in an industry where negotiating and sales skills are appallingly low, female agents usually rank more highly. WARNING: The agents who sell the most properties in an area are not necessarily the best agents. Indeed, many times, the biggest are not the best but the worst – at least when it comes

to negotiating the best price for owners. Therefore, it is important that sellers interview several agents and choose the one who is clearly a skilled negotiator. In 2016, I wrote a course for agents called "Real Estate Negotiation" and released a booklet, 42 Rules of Modern Real Estate Negotiation. To receive a copy of that booklet, please email support@jenman.com.au.

REASON 75

47. John Luce, principal of Century 21, West Pennant Hills. Circa 1994.

REASON 76

48. As told to author by the principal of Raine & Horne, Auburn. Circa 1990.

REASON 80

49. The Insider's Guide to Saving Thousands at Auction by Patrick Bright. Brolga Publishing, 2007. ISBN: 9781921221231.

50. In his 2004 book Real Estate Myths Exploded, buyers' agent David Morrell wrote: "In my role as a buyer's (sic) advocate, I estimate that 70–80 per cent of properties are sold below their true value." Chapter 1, page 9.

51. WARNING TO INEXPERIENCED INVESTORS

Some buyers' agents "double-dip". They get huge commissions from property developers which are "loaded" onto the price of the properties. The buyers' agents then tell investors they will "source" the best properties. That's not true. The buyers then pay these dodgy buyers' agents another commission and are then sold properties that can be worth hundreds of thousands of dollars LESS than the price the trusting buyers paid. Some of these buyers' agents appear respectable. Some are described as "ethical" by researchers who are "in bed" with them.

If you want to buy an investment property, buy at auction. As an investor, you can often buy good properties under market value at auctions. You will never buy properties from developers under market value. Developers are ruthless about selling for the highest price. That's why they often sell through dodgy buyers' agents, not auctions.

Who can you trust in the property investing world? Trust yourself to buy well at auction. And trust the property investment adviser Margaret Lomas. Unlike many advisers, researchers, authors and agents, Margaret Lomas cannot be bought. Her integrity is not for sale. She has many excellent books on investing. Her latest (and one of her best) is called: 20 MUST ASK QUESTIONS FOR EVERY PROPERTY INVESTOR. You can buy it at jenman.com.au.

REASON 81

52. When I opened a real estate office, I approached the Public Trust Office (in Parramatta) and showed them evidence of how I had bought their properties at public auction and then, in many cases, instantly re-sold them with an agent through private negotiation for thousands of dollars more. They were aghast. Sure, in many cases, I renovated the homes before re-selling them, but it was the ones that I immediately re-sold in the same condition for far more than the price I paid at auction that shocked them. I said, "As you are supposed to be looking after the financial affairs of the deceased, don't you have an obligation to sell their real estate for the best possible price (even if many of the estates you manage are where people have died 'intestate')?" They agreed. We were then appointed as the agent to sell several Public Trustee homes. We always got the best price because we never auctioned.

REASON 82

53. Real Estate Institute of Victoria, Auction Interest Group Seminar. Topic: "What Do You Say to the Vendor when the Purchaser is About to Sign the Contract and Has a Bank Cheque For More Than the 10%? (Meaning he/she would have paid more)".

REASON 84

54. Sotheby's, New York, April 2004. The Maurice F Neville Collection. $50,000 USD. (BHP – $127,500.) Bought with assistance of Tim Johns, James Cummins, Madison Avenue, New York.

    LONDON, Jack. Autograph manuscript signed ("Jack London") of The Game, his novel about boxing, 119 pages (10 x 8in.; 257 x 200mm), (Oakland), September 1904, in ink on rectos only of lined sheets, a working (first draft) with extensive revisions, some passages not used in the book edition (including the final sentence of the manuscript); a few margins slightly frayed, some minor soiling, but in very good condition. Blue half morocco slipcase.

55. Christie's New York. Wednesday 27 October 1999. LA Times, 28 October 1999. As reported: Asked why he spent a small fortune on the dress, co-owner Robert Schargin told reporters: "Because it wasn't $3 million, which we thought it was worth. We stole it."

    It seems the buyer was right about the dress being a steal. In 2016, the dress was re-sold to Ripley's Believe it or Not for $4.8 million (again at auction and, again, likely undersold).

56. Sydney, 20 November 1999.

57. Sotheby's, London. 10 July 2002. Sold for £49.5 million to Canadian businessman Kenneth Thomson, 2nd Baron Thomson of Fleet.

REASON 85

58. The Scotsman. Monday 15 January 2018. "Everything you need to know about buying a house at a property auction in Scotland".
59. Throughout the 1980s, the News Ltd papers, especially the Daily Telegraph in Sydney, used to publish tips for consumers about real estate advertising. One of their tips said (something such as): "Always display a price. Research shows that properties advertised without a price attract considerably less interest." But when agents started to promote more auctions, News Ltd removed the information about displaying a price (almost certainly at the behest of agents). As all agents know, advertisements are one of the many tools used by agents to condition owners down in price. Advertisements are not primarily used to attract buyers.

REASON 87

60. From as far back as 1996, I have sought the opinion of several lawyers. All agree that, in the case of most auctions, agents are in breach of their fiduciary duty to "act in the best interests" of their vendor. All it needs is for one (or more) seller/s to commence action against their agent for failing to act in their best interests and it is almost certain that a court, presented with just some of the evidence in this book, would, at least, require the agent to refund their commission. In the best-case scenario (or worst case for the agent) the court would rule that the agent also had to pay the sellers the amount by which their home had been undersold due to the agent's negligence in recommended the sellers sell by public auction. Sellers interested in pursuing this option are invited to contact the author.

A PERSONAL MESSAGE FROM NEIL JENMAN

Thank you for reading my book. If ever you are selling any property, I hope you will contact me and let me help you get the best result for yourself.

All my working life, I have been helping home-sellers achieve three goals:

First, the HIGHEST possible price.

Second, the LOWEST possible costs.

Third, the LEAST stress.

As you have read in this book, for years I devoted my life to teaching agents how to improve their businesses by improving the conditions they offered their clients. It has been a hard task. Trying to teach agents to treat clients well can be like trying to teach crabs to walk straight.

Since I wrote my first book, *Real Estate Mistakes* back in 2000 (updated edition due soon), I have been overwhelmed by the positive and appreciative response from real estate consumers.

In 2020, I switched my major focus from teaching agents to supporting consumers. I now devote most of my real estate life to working with my wonderful team (including my son Alec and my daughter Haley) at Jenman Support to help and support sellers through the entire sales process - from finding the best agent to moving out of their home. We support you all the way. Home-sellers love it. We NEVER ask you for any money nor do we ask you to sign anything, but we always protect your best interests and show you how to get the best result.

So, if you need a good agent to sell your home for the highest price with the lowest cost -including **NO UPFRONT COSTS** and **NO LOCKED-IN CONTRACTS,** you only need to take one action. Contact me or any of my colleagues anytime by calling...

PUBLICATIONS

Don't Sign Anything

Real Estate Mistakes

Help For Home-sellers

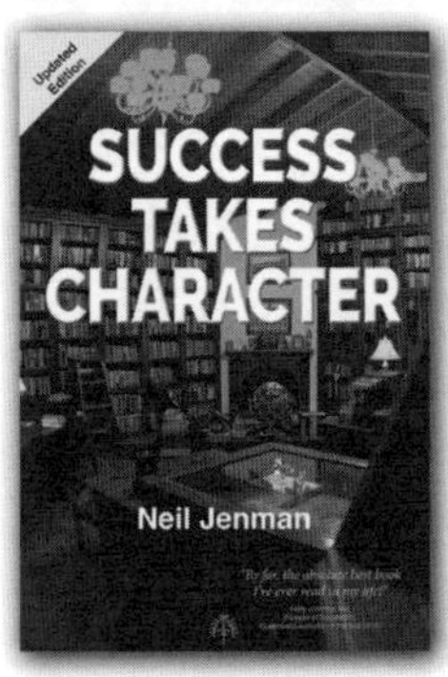

Success Takes Character

18 Worst Mistakes

13 Worst Mistakes

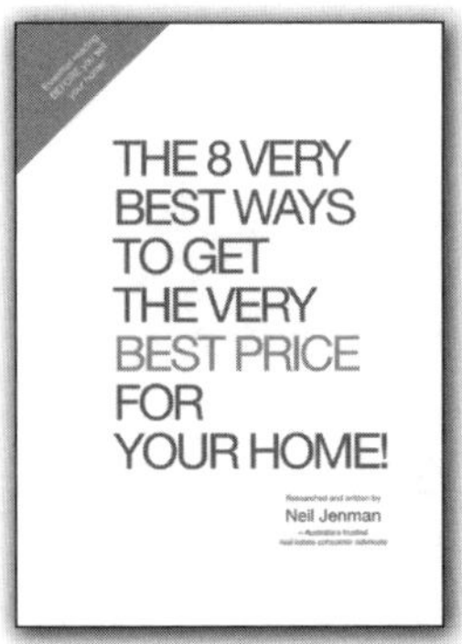

The 8 Very Best Ways

42 Rules of Negotiation

ABOUT THE AUTHOR

NEIL JENMAN entered the real estate industry in 1972 as a junior office boy in in the Central Queensland coastal town of Yeppoon. After a few months, he moved to Sydney.

In 1984 he opened a real estate office in Auburn, in Sydney's west. He rejected common systems and designed his own methods based on ethics and client care. His office became so successful that many agents began visiting him, eager to learn his ways. This led to Neil writing systems and holding seminars for thousands of agents. In the early 90s he sold his real estate office and became a full-time real estate educator. Neil travelled the world researching and speaking about real estate. Since 2000 he has written several books including the enormously popular Real Estate Mistakes, which has surpassed more than a million copies printed. It is considered the "must-read-book" for anyone buying or selling real estate.

Neil is a strong campaigner for the rights of real estate consumers and has given thousands of media interviews. He is well respected for his ethical stance and fierce protection of consumers.

Together with a dedicated team including his wife, Reiden, his son Alec, and his daughter Haley, Neil now heads up Jenman Support, a service that protects home-sellers by helping them find agents who adhere to eight protection points.

More information is available at
www.jenman.com.au.
Or 1800 1800 18.

Neil's goal is for all real estate consumers to be protected. To this end, he urges all sellers and buyers to contact 'JENMAN SUPPORT' before contacting any agent.

Neil and his wife Reiden, and another son, Harry, spend most of their time at 'Alchera', their cattle station in Central Queensland where they regularly welcome friends, many of whom are happy home-sellers.

Aside from his family, Neil's great loves are reading – especially W Somerset Maugham – spending time with friends and, despite the struggle, writing books such as Success Takes Character, his first non-real estate book which is described by Hetty Johnston (Queenslander of the Year 2015) as: "By far, the best book I've ever read in my life." He is currently working on several books.

Neil can be contacted via Jenman Support
at support@jenman.com.au.